LES ETRUSQUES
DIE ETRUSKER
THE ETRUSCANS

In the same series:

ANATOLIA I (From the origins to the end of the 2nd millennium B.C.)	U. Bahadır Alkım, Professor at the University of Istanbul
ANATOLIA II (From the 1st millennium B.C. to the end of the Roman period.)	Henri Metzger, Professor at the University of Lyons
BYZANTIUM	Antoine Bon, Professor at the University of Lyons
CELTS AND GALLO-ROMANS	Jean-Jacques Hatt, Professor at the University of Strasbourg
CENTRAL AMERICA	Claude Baudez, Research Professor at the Centre National de Recherches Scientifiques (C.N.R.S.), Paris
CENTRAL ASIA	Aleksandr Belenitsky, Professor at the Archaeological Institute of Leningrad
CHINA	Madeleine Paul-David, Professor at the Ecole du Louvre, Paris
CRETE	Nicolas Platon, former Superintendent of Antiquities, Crete; Director of the Acropolis Museum, Athens
CYPRUS	Vassos Karageorgis, Director of the Archaeological Museum, Nicosia
EGYPT	Jean Leclant, Professor at the Sorbonne, Paris
GREECE I (Mycenaean and geometric periods)	Nicolas Platon, former Superintendent of Antiquities, Crete; Director of the Acropolis Museum, Athens
GREECE II (Post-geometric periods)	François Salviat, Professor at the University of Aix-en-Provence
INDIA	Maurizio Taddei, Inspector of Oriental Art and Archaeology, Rome
INDOCHINA	Bernard P. Groslier, Curator of Historical Monuments, Angkor; Director of Archaeological Research at the Ecole Française d'Extrême-Orient
INDONESIA	Bernard P. Groslier, Curator of Historical Monuments, Angkor; Director of Archaeological Research at the Ecole Française d'Extrême-Orient
MESOPOTAMIA	Jean-Claude Margueron, Agrégé of the University; Member of the French Institute of Archaeology of Beirut

MEXICO	Jacques Soustelle
PERSIA I (From the origins to the Achaemenids)	Jean-Louis Huot, Agrégé of the University, Member of the French Institute of Archaeology of Beirut
PERSIA II (From the Seleucids to the Sassanids)	Vladimir Lukonin, Curator at the Hermitage Museum, Leningrad
PERU	Rafael Larco Hoyle †, Director of the Rafael Larco Herrera Museum, Lima
PREHISTORY	Denise de Sonneville-Bordes, Ph. D.
ROME	Gilbert Picard, Professor at the Sorbonne, Paris
SOUTHERN CAUCASUS	Boris B. Piotrovsky, Director of the Hermitage Museum, Leningrad
SOUTHERN SIBERIA	Mikhail Gryaznov, Professor at the Archaeological Institute of Leningrad
SYRIA-PALESTINE I (Ancient Orient)	Jean Perrot, Head of the French Archaeological Mission in Israel
SYRIA-PALESTINE II (Classical Orient)	Michael Avi Yonah, Professor at the Hebrew University of Jerusalem
THE TEUTONS	R. Hachmann, Professor at the University of Saarbrücken
URARTU	Boris B. Piotrovsky, Director of the Hermitage Museum, Leningrad

ANCIENT CIVILIZATIONS

Series prepared under the direction of
Jean Marcadé, Professor of Archaeology
at the University of Bordeaux

THE ANCIENT CIVILIZATION OF

THE ETRUSCANS

RAYMOND BLOCH

Translated from the French by JAMES HOGARTH

61 illustrations in colour; 71 illustrations in black and white

COWLES BOOK COMPANY, INC.
488 MADISON AVENUE
NEW YORK, N.Y. 10022

Printed in Switzerland

CONTENTS

PREFACE

Archaeology presents very diverse characteristics in different parts of the world. It is the object of this series to analyse the specific features of archaeological research in the different areas where it is active, and to examine the differing conditions in which this young but ambitious science is perfecting its methods and achieving its results.

For modern archaeology has become a science. The problems with which it has to deal differ from area to area, but it seeks everywhere to formulate them with precision, to tackle them methodically, and gradually to achieve their solution by an exact and accurate interpretation of the results of research. Discovery is no longer left to the operation of chance, and archaeology is no longer concerned merely to supply the museums with "good pieces". It seeks to collaborate with anthropology, ethnography, philology, and above all with history; for it can check and complement all aspects of history—political, social, economic and religious as well as cultural. Archaeology has taken its place—last, perhaps, but not least—among the human sciences.

The change is most striking in the case of Etruria. True, Tuscany is still a land of fabulous tombs, of patient collectors, of ingenious counterfeiters. But the great aim of contemporary Etruscan archaeology is to solve the enigma of Etruscan origins and the mystery of the language, to throw light on the pattern of trade in the Mediterranean in ancient times, and to establish the historical facts about the relations between the Etruscans and the Latins.

In the systematic exploration of the soil ever greater use is being made of the resources and equipment made available by the latest techniques. First there was air photography; and now geophysical methods have found new uses and made their contribution to the progress of archaeology in this part of Italy. Sensational results have been achieved by the engineers of the Lerici

Foundation with the help of resistivity curves, patterns of magnetic anomalies and seismic diagrams, supplemented by the stratigraphic, the periscopic and the photographic probes. Etruria has become a fascinating testing ground for new archaeological methods.

J.M.

We are indebted to Professor Mario Moretti, Superintendent of Antiquities for Southern Etruria and Director of the Villa Giulia Museum in Rome, for his ready cooperation and invaluable assistance. We are also grateful to Professor Boris Piotrovsky, Director of the Hermitage Museum in Leningrad, who allowed us to reproduce some of the Etruscan material in his care.

We should also like to thank Mrs A. Voshchinina, Keeper of the Etrusco-Roman section of the Hermitage Museum, and Sig. U. Calace, Assistant in the Superintendency of Antiquities for Southern Etruria, for the help they so readily gave us.

Finally, our thanks are due to Dr Luciano Merlo of Rome for his aid and support throughout the production of this work.

THE HISTORY OF ETRUSCOLOGY

I

There are some peoples who have particularly aroused the interest both of scholars and of the general public; and among them the Etruscans undoubtedly take a high place. This interest is easily explained by the strange and splendid destiny which was theirs, in that area in the heart of Italy to which they have left their name. By the beginning of the 7th century B.C. they had built up a brilliant and promising civilisation, and they came within an ace of unifying the whole of the Italian peninsula under their control. But Italy was destined to be Roman, not Etruscan. The Etruscans were early in the field, but their power was to be short-lived. After some two and a half centuries of prosperity and success came a rapid decline which steadily diminished their ambitions. In spite of the most determined resistance the great Tuscan cities succumbed one after the other to the repeated hammer-blows of the Roman legions. By the middle of the 3rd century B.C. Etruria had lost its independence and was already politically integrated into Roman Italy.

Despite the briefness of their career the Etruscans left behind them countless records of their presence and their activity. Some of the richest museums in Italy are filled with the works of art they created or imported from Greece and the East by the sea trade routes: think, for example, of the National Museum of the Villa Giulia in Rome, the Etruscan Museum in the Vatican, and the Archaeological Museum in Florence. And the soil of Tuscany still conceals vast numbers of tombs, built of stone or hewn from the tufa, in which the dead were deposited along with the offerings of grave goods which were to meet their needs in the life beyond.

In this book we shall begin by following the development of archaeological research in Tuscany up to the present day; we shall then consider what problems still remain, and what methods are being applied in the attempt to solve them; and finally we shall discuss the significance of the latest results.

The interest which the ancients took in the history and civilisation of Etruria, which so briefly occupied a place in the interplay of the Mediterranean powers, is clearly attested by the number of allusions in Greek and Roman writers. And, as we should expect, this interest was accompanied by a marked appreciation of the surviving remains of Etruscan art, which were no doubt handed down from father to son in the great families of Tuscany, and were constantly being revealed by chance discoveries. And in fact we learn from some lines of Horace that Etruscan bronze statuettes were much in favour with art lovers. He writes in one of his *Epistles* (II, 2, 180): *gemmas, marmor, ebur, Tyrrhena sigilla, tabellas, argentum, vestes Gaetulo murice tinctas, sunt qui non habeant, est qui non curat habere.*

"Precious stones, marble, ivory, Tyrrhenian statuettes, pictures, silver, fabrics dyed with the purple of Gaetulia: there are men who have none of these; I know one man who cares not for any of them."

In this famous passage Horace is citing a number of superfluous objects which can be acquired by those who have money, and are frequently used for ostentatious display; adding, in his role as moralist, that a man can live without them and indeed will never miss them. It has perhaps not been sufficiently noted how revealing this reference is about the high esteem in which the ancients held these delicate products of Etruscan art. Horace puts them in the same category as precious stones, ivory and silver; and no doubt the connoisseurs of antiquity sought after them with no less keenness than the collectors of today. We may reasonably suppose that the same applied to all the jewels and delicate decorative objects produced by the workshops of Tuscany.

The Middle Ages, concerned above all with tradition, to some extent lost the sense of history—only Rome, perhaps, continuing to exert some influence through the memory of her greatness. But the Renaissance sought to return to the direct sources of knowledge about antiquity, to its literature and its monuments. The still visible remains of Imperial Rome provided matter for the descriptions, as well as an object for the enthusiasm, of the humanists of the 15th and 16th centuries. Already we find among the artists of the period—the architects, the sculptors, the painters—an interest in archaeological study and in investigation on the ground, even though the contemporary efforts in this field were devoid of any scientific spirit. Already, too, the fruitful soil of Tuscany was beginning to yield some of the great bronzes which are now the pride of the Archaeological Museum in Florence—the Chimaera of Arezzo, the Minerva from the same town, and the famous statue of the *Arringatore* or Orator, which were found one after the other in the middle of the 16th century.

The impetus thus given was never lost, and men of later periods continued to pursue their researches and to travel the roads—then wild and almost deserted—in the countryside round Tarquinia, Siena and Chiusi. The size of the Etruscan cemeteries and the structure of the tombs, preserving intact the treasures entrusted to them, promised a far richer harvest than could be looked for anywhere else. There was, of course, no idea of proper archaeological methods; but virgin tombs could be found easily enough by relying on the flair and experience of the local inhabitants, who knew every yard of the countryside and could detect the passages—hewn from the tufa of the plateaux and hillsides and then filled in with earth—which led infallibly to the entrances of the tombs. In the 17th century some of the fine painted tombs of Tarquinia came to light, revealing to the wondering gaze of their finders paintings which had not been seen for a thousand years.

The wastage was considerable. Anything that was not seen to have an assured market value was destroyed or cast aside. Nevertheless so much valuable material found its way into various collections that the need was felt to draw up the first catalogues. Between 1616 and 1619 a Scottish scholar, Thomas Dempster, compiled a large work in seven books on ancient Etruria under the title *De Etruria regali libri septem*, which was not published until a century later. This work, full of uncritical learning but also of imagination, contained a fine series of 93 plates reproducing the most famous Etruscan archaeological remains of the period. This first corpus of knowledge, modest as it was, nevertheless pointed the way to the great catalogues of later periods.

The publication of *De Etruria regali* at Florence in 1723 marked the beginning of an unprecedented wave of enthusiasm for Etruria and its people among the learned men of the day. Etruscan civilisation was given an important place—sometimes a quite exaggerated place—in the history of antiquity. The Etruscans came to be regarded as cousins to the Hebrews, and were thought to have anticipated the Greeks in the development of their splendid art. None of this, of course, stands up to examination: all these theories were no more than flights of fancy without any scientific basis. But it is easy to see how this *etruscheria*, this Etruscomania of the 18th century, developed under the powerful stimulus given by the discovery, in the very heart of Italy, of works of art of such outstanding quality, and by the exotic and mysterious character of the civilisation which was thus revealed.

But in spite of these extravagances a beginning was made with the bringing together of valuable factual data about the Etruscans. On 29th December 1726 the Etruscan Academy of Cortona was founded by Onofrio Baldelli. By a pleasant conceit the President of the Academy was given the Etruscan title of *Lucumo*, his term of office being democratically limited to a year. Forty citizens of Cortona and a hundred other gentlemen made up the membership of the Academy, which met twice a month for the learned discussions known as the *Notti Coritane*. At these meetings communications and memoirs were read and the latest discoveries reported, and this was followed by animated discussion, conducted in a tone of perfect courtesy which later scholars were not always able to maintain. Today, more than two centuries after its foundation, the Academy of Cortona is still in existence, providing a remarkable example of continuity and perseverance. It is still possible to read with pleasure, and perhaps with a responsive thrill, the nine handsome volumes which it published between 1738 and 1795 under the elegant and harmonious title of *Saggi di dissertazioni accademiche pubblicamente lette nella nobile Accademia etrusca dell'antichissima città di Cortona.*

The excavations which were now carried out at the various sites were the starting point of some of the Etruscan museums which were to increase in number, as the years went by, in the area between Rome and Florence. Thus a fortunate discovery in the extreme north of Tuscany, near the fine city of Volterra, revealed the monumental tomb of the great family of Caecina, and the forty cinerary urns which it contained formed the first collection of the Archaeological Museum of Volterra, founded in 1750 by the prelate Mario Guarnacci and still attracting tourists with its wealth of material. These first archaeological finds at Volterra, like those at Cortona, were published by a Florentine, Antonio Francesco Gori, whose work was excellently done by the standards of the time and is still consulted today. Another source which is still useful is the series of sketches by a Scottish artist, James Byres, a friend of Piranesi, which record, in an elegant and only slightly romanticised form, the discovery of some of the painted tombs of Tarquinia. Byres's work was not published until the following century, in 1842, when it appeared in London under the title *Hypogaei, or the sepulchral caverns of Tarquinia.* It has the particular merit of preserving some of the Tarquinian paintings which have since disappeared.

The great engraver of this period, Piranesi, was greatly attracted by the art of the Etruscans, and was concerned in particular with the influence of this art on Rome. In 1761 he published a large work entitled *Della magnificenza ed architettura dei Romani*, designed to exalt the achievements of the Latin genius and the architects of Rome. In discussing the origins of Roman art he attached great—perhaps excessive—importance to the presence and influence of the Etruscans. His very fine etchings reconstruct Roman buildings of the period of the Tarquins, such as the Cloaca Maxima and the temple on the Capitol. But there is still much of interest in his defence of a national style of art in ancient Italy which was first Etruscan and later Roman. After a dispute with the Frenchman Jean-Paul Mariette, who sought to deny all originality to Etruria and attributed everything to the influence of Greece, Piranesi developed his own ideas further in a second book, published in 1765, *Della introduzione e del progresso delle Belle Arti in Europa nei tempi antichi.* This contained many fine plates showing tombs recently discovered at Tarquinia and Chiusi.

All this activity contributed to the building up of public interest in the problems posed by Etruscan civilisation. The most learned man of the day, however—Winckelmann—gave only a restricted place to Etruria in his massive works of synthesis. On the other hand, the Comte de Caylus, in his *Recueil d'Antiquités égyptiennes, grecques, étrusques et romaines,* gave a prominent place to Tuscan art. In this work he shows a very proper caution, realising clearly that in the then existing state of knowledge it was often extremely difficult to decide on the exact origin of a work of art. "We are not in a position," he says modestly, "to distinguish the work of these different peoples, since we have not sufficient pieces for comparison." In this he shows the attitude of the true scholar. And we must admit that even today it is difficult to recognise the place of manufacture of certain archaic bronzes, which are as likely to have come from a Greek workshop in Magna Graecia or Sicily as from an Etruscan city. We shall return to this kind of problem in a later chapter.

Nevertheless, one of the great problems raised by the archaeological material yielded in such quantity by the Etruscan tombs was about to be definitively settled. These tombs contained, along with other objects from different

1

2

3

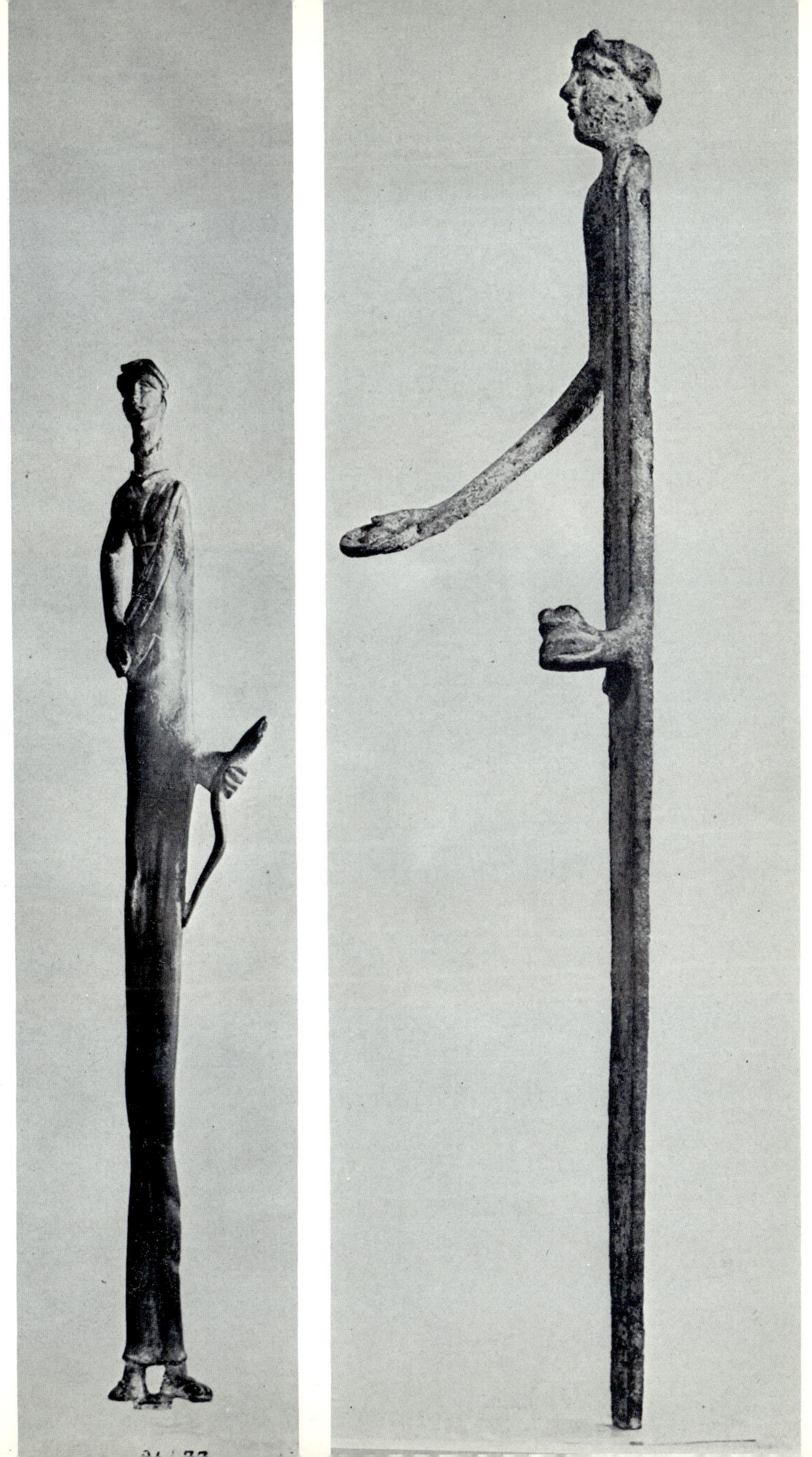

4

5

6

7

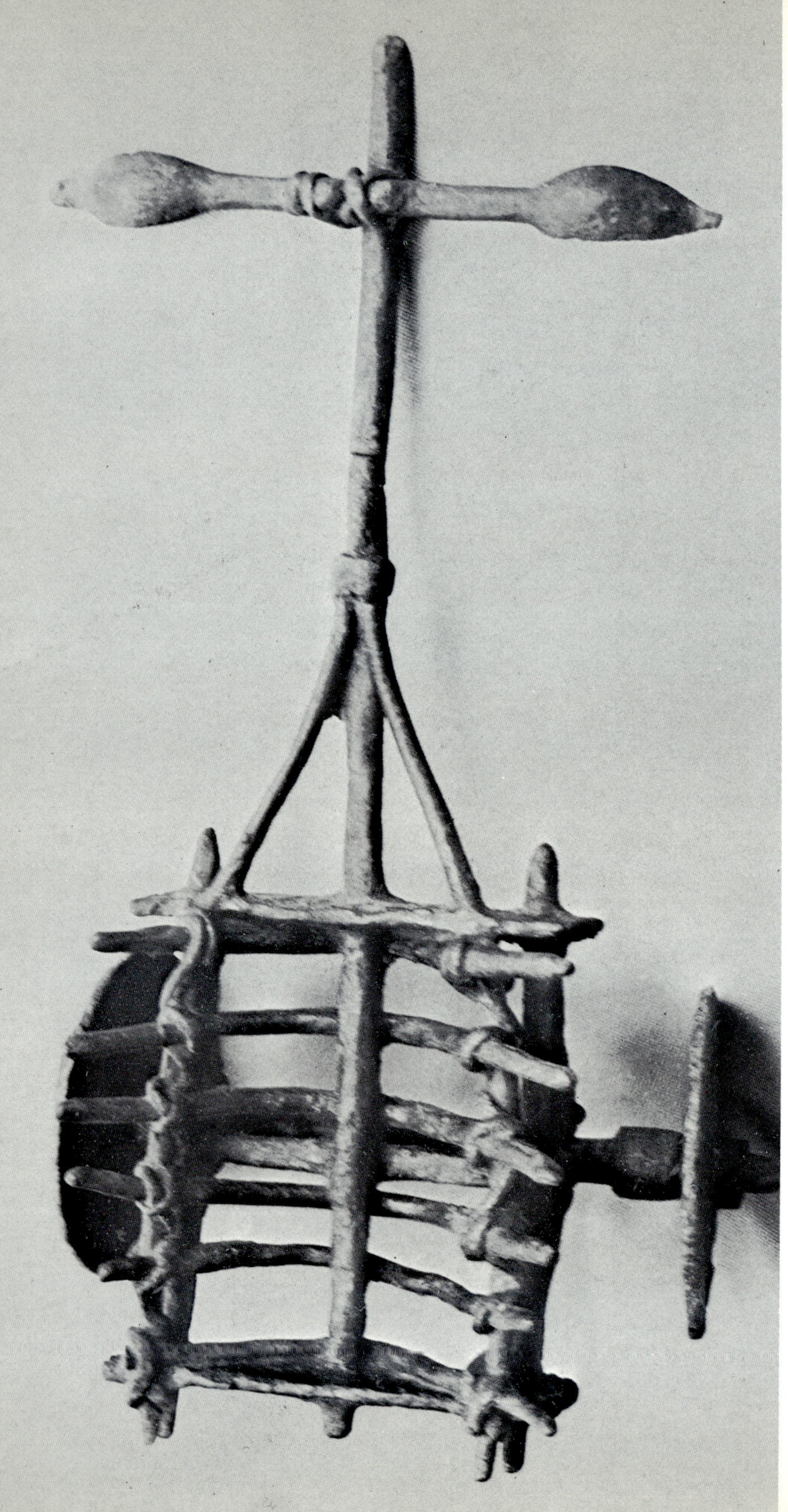

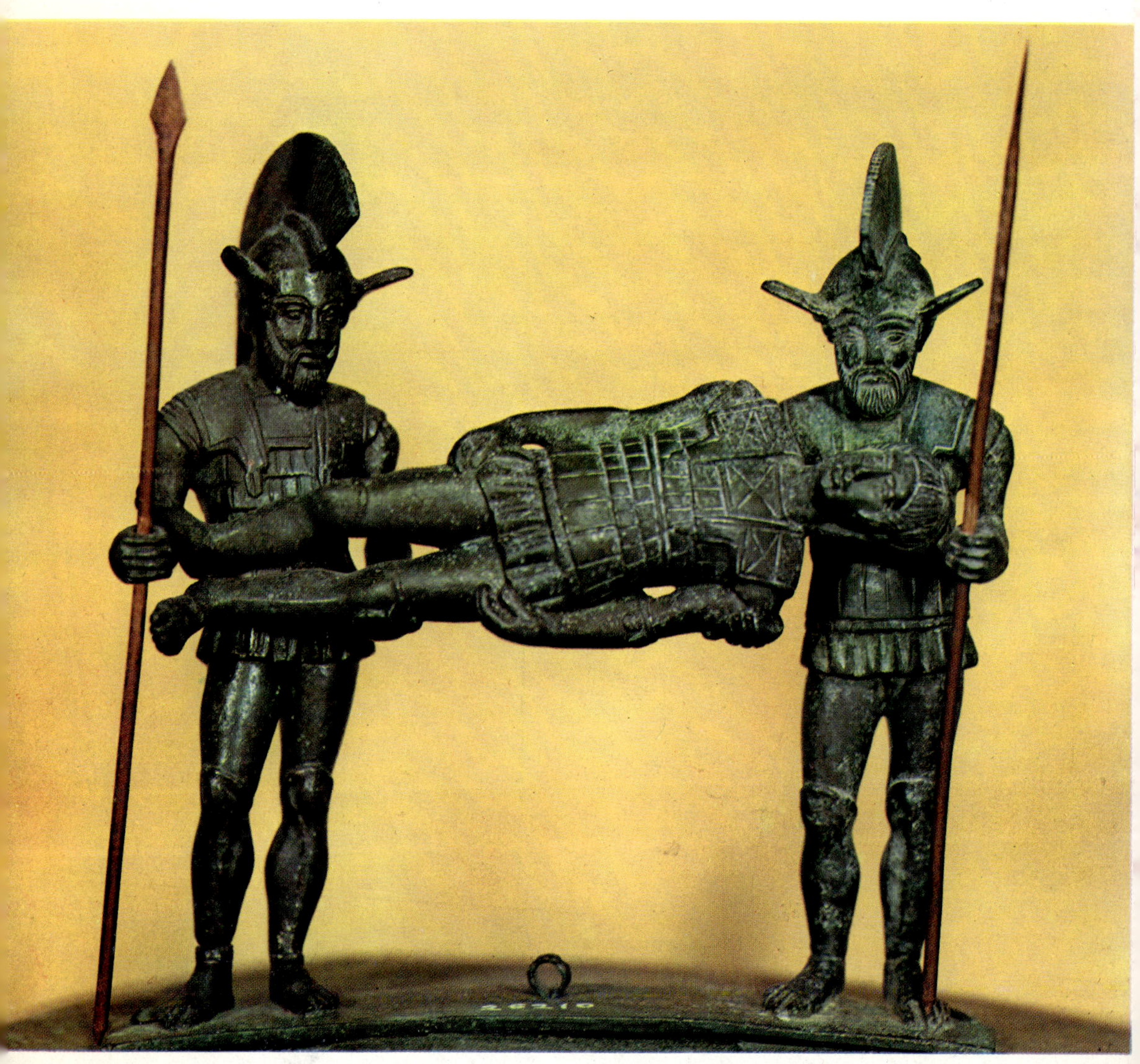

10

11 →

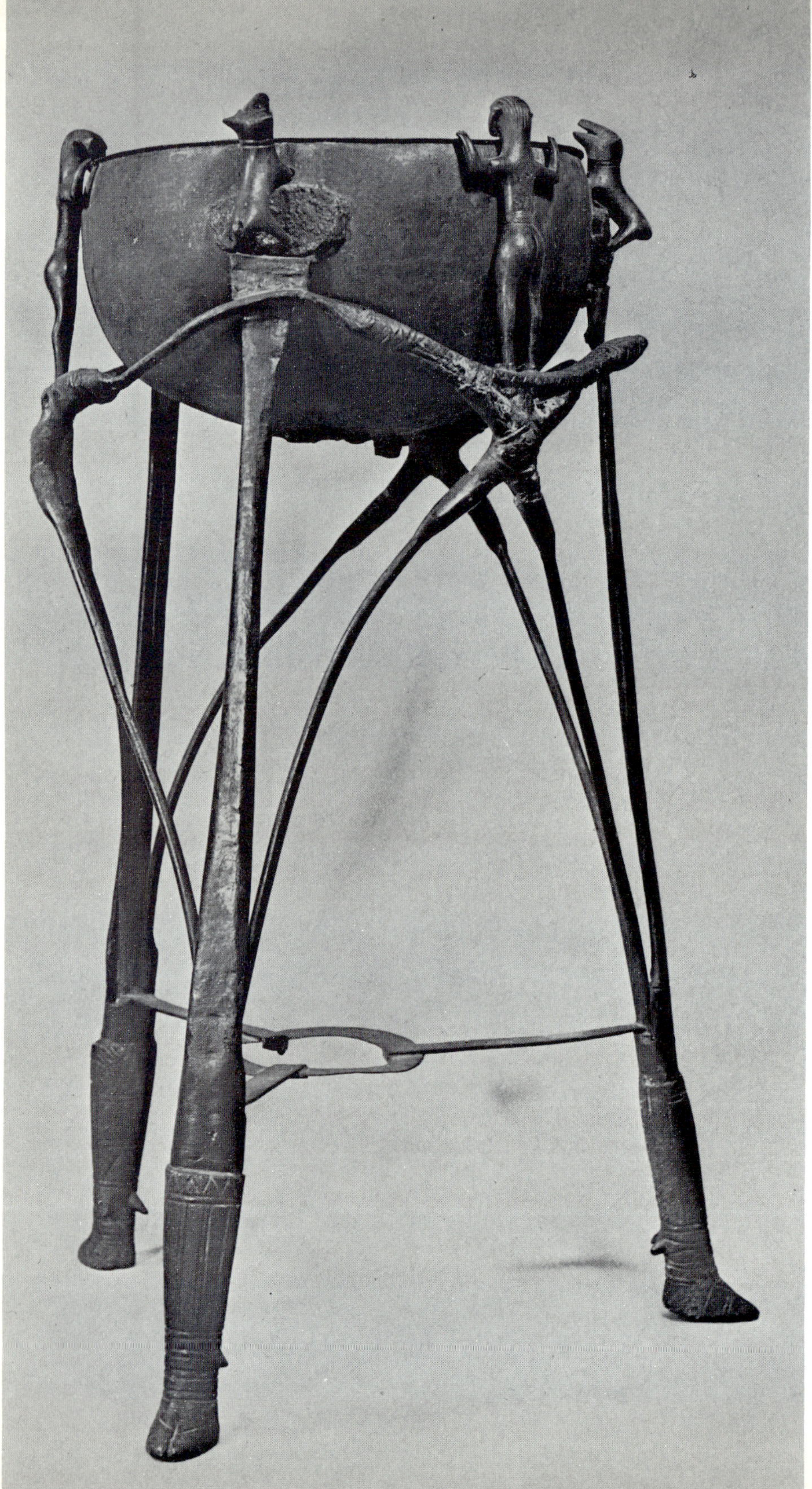

16

17

18

19

20

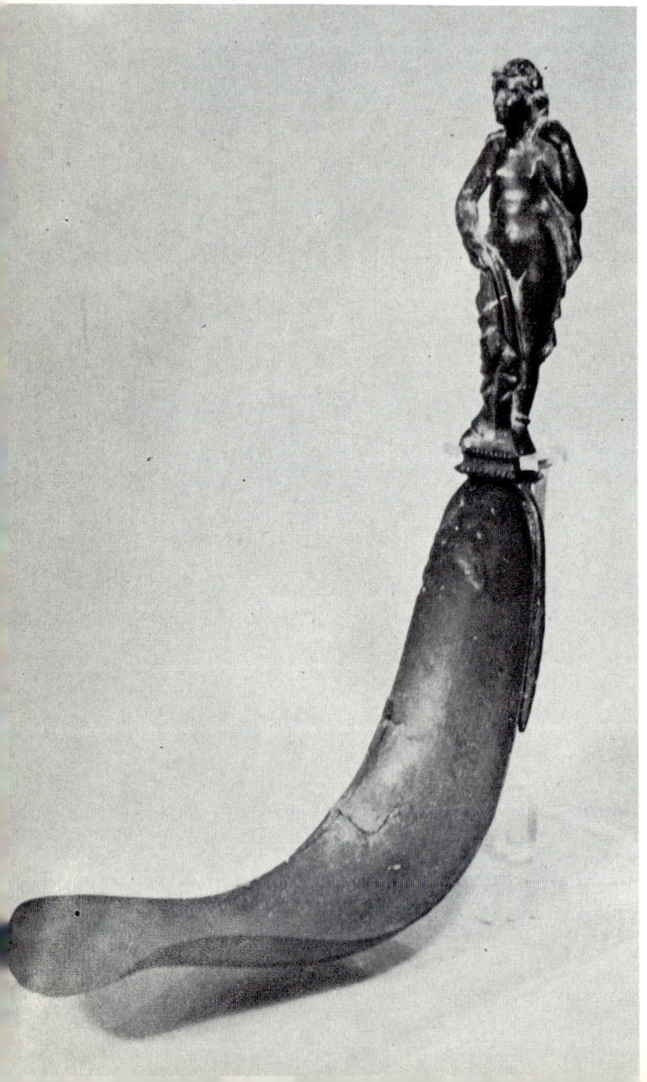

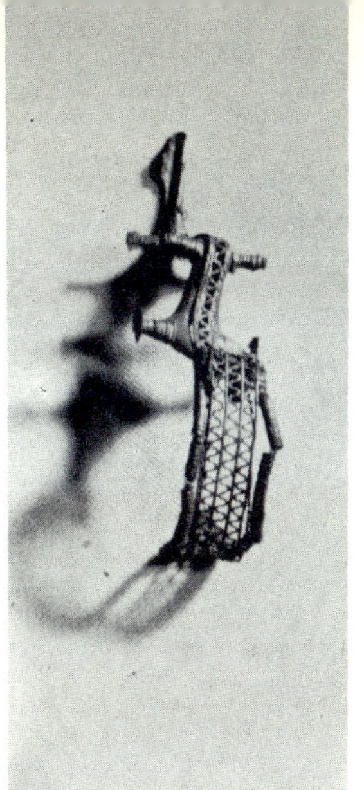

21

22

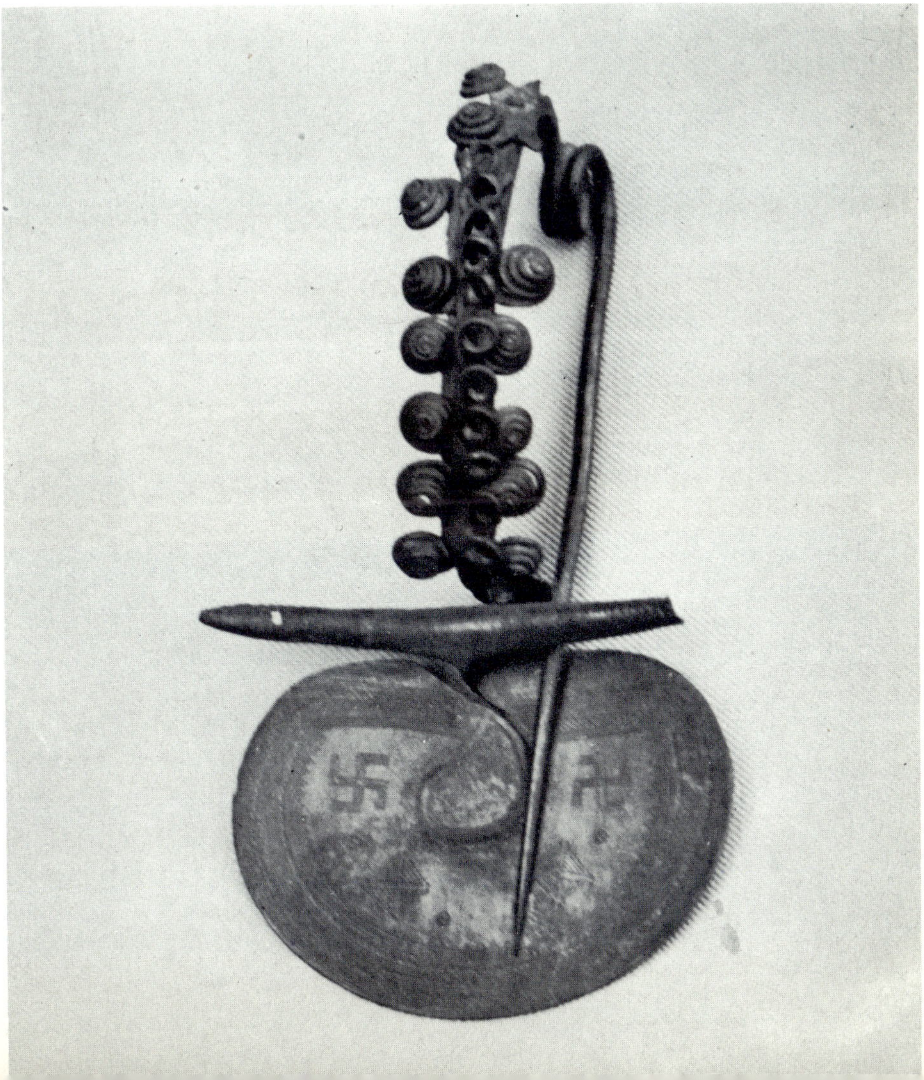

23

25

26→

sources, very large quantities of Greek terracotta vases, decorated in the earliest period with figures painted in black on the red background of the clay, and from the beginning of the 5th century B.C. onwards with red figures framed in a black painted background. These figured vases are found in a great variety of shapes, and are decorated with scenes from daily life and a great range of episodes from the epic stories of the Greek gods and heroes. These graceful works by skilled craftsmen are often of great beauty, and were sought after in ancient times as they are today by collectors and museums. The great works of Greek painting have, for all practical purposes, disappeared; and these vases sometimes preserve for us imitations of the lost works of Polygnotus or Zeuxis. They are also valuable evidence on trade relations between different countries and exchanges between one area and another. And finally they are a most useful means for dating complex archaeological structures; for the experts can now date these Greek vases with great precision, and when one of them appears alongside objects which are difficult to date by themselves—as is often the case with Etruscan objects—it provides a most valuable point of reference.

The Etruscans were great admirers of Greek vases and imported them in vast quantities. Their orders, indeed, were on such a large scale that in the cemeteries of the city of Vulci alone—thanks to the excellent protection afforded by the structure of the chamber tombs—more black-figured Greek vases have been discovered than at Athens itself where they were produced. It was this incredible abundance that led to a fundamental misunderstanding about these vases in the 18th century. As a result of inadequate knowledge of Greek art and a lack of familiarity with the products of specifically Tuscan art, these delicate creations by Greek craftsmen were taken for Etruscan work. This error undoubtedly explains the title of *Le Vase étrusque* which Prosper Mérimée gave to one of his best known short stories; and Goethe records a piece of direct evidence on the fashion for Greek vases, thus erroneously considered to be Etruscan, when he writes in his *Italienische Reise* (published in 1787):" The price of Etruscan vases is now very high... Every traveller wants to possess one".

Already, however, Winckelmann, with an archaeological sense ahead of his time, had realised the mistake and established the truth. At the beginning of the following century an intelligent priest, Luigi Lanzi, finally refuted the error which had become so firmly rooted in the mind of his contemporaries, in a dissertation published at Florence in 1806 under the significant title *Dei vasi antichi dipinti volgarmente chiamati etruschi.* In this he finally established the distinction between Greek and Etruscan pottery, an achievement for which all later students must be grateful and which earns him a place among the pioneers of Etruscology.

The 19th century marked a decisive stage in the history of our subject. After the learned studies of the princely courts and academies of the 18th century, the Romantic period saw an upsurge of passionate interest in archaeological research; and almost everywhere a strange new fascination was exerted on men's minds by the East. Napoleon's campaign in Egypt inflamed all imaginations—even though the Emperor was reported to have said, somewhat uncharitably, that at the battle of the Pyramids he had placed his timid scholars in the centre of the square formed by his battalions, along with the donkeys. Oriental studies were about to be born, and soon a series of sensational discoveries was to open up new knowledge and fresh perspectives.

This new passion for the exotic and for the remains of the dead past took on an almost mystical aspect in the Romantic poets of the northern countries, and Etruria became one of the main objects of this new interest. A number of scholars and *dilettanti*, mainly German, met in Rome about the year 1820 and formed the group known as the Hyperboreans; and three members of the group, E. Gerhard, A. Kestner, and the Baron von Stackelberg, were to give a decisive impulsion to archaeological research in Tuscany. This was followed by the establishment of the Istituto di Corrispondenza

Archeologica, which enjoyed the support of Prince Frederick of Prussia and was to have a long and illustrious career.

But this scholarly interest was accompanied by feverish activity on the part of the great landowners, on whose property the peasants were accidentally discovering tombs which were still intact. From 1828 onwards Napoleon's younger brother Lucien Bonaparte, Prince of Canino, who owned the site of the cemeteries of Vulci—probably the richest area, archaeologically, in the whole of Italy—began excavating there on his own account. The spoils were enormous, and his collection was rapidly enriched by thousands of Greek vases and Etruscan jewellery and bronzes. These fantastic discoveries made a great impression on the public mind; and it created a sensation in Roman society when the Princess of Canino appeared at a reception at the Papal court in 1830 splendidly decked in jewels recently discovered on her property. Many of the new finds were sold to collectors in different countries, and are now to be seen scattered about in museums throughout the world. But from the scientific point of view the losses were irreparable. The excavations were of course conducted with a complete disregard for scientific principles, and no excavation records were kept. In consequence there is nothing to show for these haphazard and purely mercenary campaigns but the finds themselves: nothing remains of the scientific data that could so easily have been recorded. And to make matters worse, objects thought to be without any market value were broken up and left lying about, to disappear forever.

The case of the Prince of Canino was not an isolated one. Businessmen like G.P. Campana extended their explorations over great areas in Etruria and gathered immense collections. Campana's collection was later to enrich many museums *(Plates 11 – 15, 131)*, including in particular the Louvre. This extraordinary period of incessant discoveries and irreparable destruction is admirably recorded in the lively book by George Dennis, *The Cities and Cemeteries of Etruria*. First published in 1848, with later editions in 1878 and 1883, this is still an essential book for the library of all concerned with Etruscan studies.

Between 1830 and 1870 some of the richest and most important tombs in Etruria were discovered, and their contents are still providing material for study whose possibilities have not yet been exhausted. Among these were the Regolini-Galassi Tomb at Cerveteri, discovered in 1836 by the arch-priest Regolini and General Galassi, whose name it bears; the Isis and François Tombs at Vulci; the monumental underground tomb of the Volumnii near Perugia, so popular with tourists, which illustrates the impressive scale of Etruscan funerary architecture in the late period; many painted tombs at Veii and Tarquinia *(Plates 76–104)*; and finally two tombs found in the delightful town of Palestrina—the Roman Praeneste, 25 miles east of Rome—the Barberini and Bernardini Tombs, which would rival the Regolini-Galassi Tomb, if indeed that tomb *could* have a rival, in the wealth of gold jewellery they contained. The discoveries at Palestrina revealed that in the 7th century B.C., while Rome was still a humble and undistinguished settlement on the Tiber, the rarest products of the Orient were reaching this city only a short distance away, as a result of the intense trading activity which linked Etruria and the eastern Mediterranean.

Almost at the same time an important discovery in the plain of the Po, not far from Bologna, revealed the existence of an Italic civilisation which had immediately preceded the Etruscan civilisation in the Po area—and also, as was soon to be realised, in Etruria itself. The result was a considerable widening of the historical perspective. The discovery was made in 1853 by Count Gozzadini when on one of his properties, at the village of Villanova, he found a cemetery containing many tombs, though with rather meagre contents. The tombs consisted of small shafts sunk in the earth containing jars of coarse terracotta shaped like two truncated cones placed base to base. These held the ashes of the dead and the crude grave goods which accompanied them. The decoration of the pottery was in geometrical patterns incised on the clay and made up of a number of simple elements—circles, triangles, dots, chevrons, and so on. There was no representation of the human figure, nor any inscription. Yet this people who cremated their dead also knew the use of iron, for among the bronze toilet articles and weapons there were also some weapons of iron. The civilisation revealed at Villanova thus belonged to the first Iron Age in Italy, and it was called Villanovan after the name of the site. Thereafter a large number of Villanovan cemeteries were identified both in the plain of the Po and in Etruria. At Rome itself and in Latium a form of culture known as "Latial" was found which is closely related to Villanovan. The question of the origin of the Etruscans thus took on quite a different aspect.

But now another new phase was beginning in the archaeological study of Etruria and the neighbouring areas. The beginning of the new phase can be dated to about 1870-1880. The necessity of rigorous excavation methods had at last become accepted, and a period was beginning in which it could be said that at last archaeology had become a science. Henceforth errors in the work of survey or excavation were no longer excusable, for archaeology had passed beyond its earlier uncertainties. In future each discovery must represent a step forward in the advance of knowledge.

Two campaigns carried out at this time were models of their kind—one by Zannoni at Bologna, the other by the Frenchman Stéphane Gsell at Vulci. The former excavated, with impeccable competence, a large Etruscan cemetery at the Charterhouse of Bologna, the necropolis of the Certosa. This demonstrated the succession, in the same area, of a Villanovan and an Etruscan civilisation, and established the basic facts on which all future historians must rely. At Vulci, too, Gsell carried out an exemplary excavation, and his report, illustrated by plans, maps and photographs, gives an exact record of the contents of each of the tombs excavated. A hundred years later these two campaigns are still useful to the modern student. The amateur had now given place to the scholar; discovery was no longer a matter of idle curiosity but was aimed at securing positive factual data, an assured starting point for historical study. The publication of results became indispensable; research now required a team rather than an individual.

The increased scale of excavation in Etruria, and indeed throughout Italy, necessarily raised problems of publication and preservation. A regular official bulletin on excavations in Italy was therefore established in 1876; it has continued to appear since then and provides a regular and valuable source for scholars. Under pressure of necessity—for more and more space was required to display and to store the objects found by excavation—the museums increased both in number and in size. The Gregorian Etruscan Museum in the Vatican, which was established as early as 1836, was to set a new standard in the size and value of its collections; but it was soon joined by the Villa Giulia Museum in Rome and the Archaeological Museum in Florence. Together these formed what might, in the peaceful world of Etruscology, be called the concert of the three Great Powers. But space was needed in the excavation areas themselves—rooms for display, cupboards for storage; and this led to the founding of the local museums which were to flourish exceedingly in later years—at Bologna, Tarquinia, Chiusi, Siena, Arezzo and elsewhere. It is useful, wherever possible, to display the results of excavation near their place of discovery, for an object in its original setting has a significance and a value which it loses if it is sent far away. Of course, regard must be had for ease of access to the public; but the steady development of tourism in our day has deprived the great cities of the privileged position which they enjoyed only a few years ago. Thus the material from the famous Celtic tomb of Vix, with its colossal bronze mixing-jar and its splendid gold torques, is scientifically displayed in the museum at Châtillon-sur-Seine, close to its place of discovery.

For the most recent period it is necessary to note only the most significant results. We shall return later to the problems of method and the prospects for the future. The most important discoveries have undoubtedly been those made over the years on the site of the large temple at Veii, the so-called Temple of Apollo. Since 1916, the memorable year when the great statue of Apollo *(Plates 28–29)* was discovered, we have seen the gradual reconstitution of a considerable part of the group of terracotta statues which decorated the roof ridge of the temple *(Plate 27)*. These are works of exceptional importance and high artistic value, dating from the very end of the 6th century B.C., when the dynasty of the Tarquins was reigning at Rome, ten miles south of Veii. This is the supreme expression of archaic Etruscan art, under Ionian influence but with its own local characteristics. We can even guess the workshop from which these statues came; for we know from Roman sources that a great sculptor from Veii, Vulca, was called to Rome for the decoration of the temple of Jupiter Capitolinus, which was dedicated in 509 B.C. While at Rome he created a famous quadriga in terracotta which formed the acroterion of the temple, as well as the statue of Jupiter himself. His skill and renown are celebrated by Varro, and clearly his fame reached far beyond the frontiers of his native city. To his workshop, therefore, we can undoubtedly attribute these figures of divinities from Veii itself representing the story of the dispute between Apollo and Heracles for the captured hind.

Since 1945 archaeological research in Etruria has taken on a new pace and a more international character. An important feature has been the spirit of cooperation and generosity which has resulted in the granting of authority to excavate to the foreign schools of archaeology based in Rome. In consequence a number of other countries have been able to join forces with the Italian School in probing the soil of Tuscany. These reinforcements have made it possible to undertake work not only in the cemeteries, as in the past, but also on the sites of the Etruscan cities. We cannot of course hope to find on these urban sites the variety of objects and the treasures concealed in the tombs; but from the point of view of the historian of Etruscan civilisation these researches are of the greatest interest. The layout of the Etruscan cities, the nature and the organisation of their defensive system, and the structure of their sanctuaries are being established with increasing clarity. The best evidence in this respect is provided by the unusually promising site of Marzabotto, a few miles south of Bologna. Discovered in 1890 by Brizio, this site has continued since then to attract the interest of archaeologists. During the last twenty years excavation has been resumed on an increased scale and with improved methods; and the results have been fully up to expectations.

This is the point at which we have now arrived. Research is being keenly pursued in a number of different places, new discoveries are constantly being reported, and historical knowledge continues to advance. Quite recently, in the summer of 1964, the excavations carried out by the Institute of Etruscology of Rome under the direction of Massimo Pallottino achieved a spectacular success. In the course of a survey of a sacred area at Pyrgi, one of the ports of the ancient Caere, four inscriptions engraved with great care on sheets of gold and bronze came to light. One of them was written in Punic *(Plate 53)*, the others in Etruscan *(Plates 51, 52)*, and all of them were dedications to the goddess worshipped in the sanctuary. These new texts contribute very substantially to our knowledge in a number of different directions: we shall have more to say about them in a later chapter.

28

29 →

30

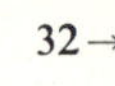

32→

31

33

34 →

35

39

40

CURRENT PROBLEMS AND UNCERTAINTIES

II

After this rapid survey of the history of Etruscology we must now sum up the present state of knowledge and see where the continual progress of archaeological research has taken us. It must be recognised at once that two important problems still remain unsolved—the origin of the Etruscans and the language they spoke; and we now consider the present state of these problems and possible means of solving them.

The question of the origin of a people is always a complex and difficult one to resolve, for it takes us back into dim and distant times for which our sources are much later and often contradictory. And yet to the ancients there was no room for doubt about the origin of the Etruscans. They were known to have come from Asia Minor at a very early date, in the 13th century before our era, and had then settled in the area which they selected as their new homeland. This is what Herodotus has to say about them: "In the days of Atys the son of Manes, there was great scarcity through the whole land of Lydia... So the king determined to divide the nation in half, and to make the two portions draw lots, the one to stay, the other to leave the land. He would continue to reign over those whose lot it should be to remain behind; the emigrants should have his son Tyrrhenus for their leader. The lot was cast, and they who had to emigrate went down to Smyrna, and built themselves ships, in which, after they had put on board all needful stores, they sailed away in search of new homes and better sustenance. After sailing past many countries they came to Umbria, where they built cities for themselves, and fixed their residence. Their former name of Lydians they laid aside, and called themselves after the name of the king's son, who led the colony, Tyrrhenians".

The story is coherent, and seemed so satisfactory to the ancients that they accepted it with hardly a dissentient voice. The Etruscans were accepted as coming from Lydia, and the peculiar characteristics of their civilisation were explained by this Anatolian origin. The Roman poets commonly referred to the Etruscans as Lydians. The only discordant voice was that of a Greek rhetor, Dionysius of Halicarnassus, who lived at Rome in the time of Augustus. He refused to accept the current opinion: "I do not think that the Tyrrhenians were colonists from Lydia," he wrote. "They have not the same language as the Lydians, and it cannot be said that they retain any other peculiarity which might come from their supposed country of origin. They do not worship the same gods as the Lydians, they do not have the same laws, and in this respect at least differ still more from the Lydians than from the Pelasgians. Thus those who say that this is not a people come from abroad but an indigenous people appear to me to be on the mark. This seems to me to follow from the fact that they are a very ancient people which resembles no other either in language or in customs."

Thus Dionysius of Halicarnassus is well aware of the individual character of Etruscan civilisation, but he sees nothing in Lydia which seems to him to correspond to these special features. He prefers, therefore, to think that the Etruscans go back to an extremely remote antiquity and are sprung from the soil of their own country. This critical spirit is highly commendable; but our knowledge of ancient Anatolia has made great strides since then, and we must ask ourselves whether it is still possible to reject the established tradition. Some scholars think it is. In their view, the story of the Etruscans' migration from beyond the sea is one of the fables of which the ancient histories are so full, and is not be considered seriously. No Anatolian dialect has been found to be related to the Etruscan language, and there is no real evidence of any kind for an Oriental origin. Like the Basques, the Etruscans must be a people of Mediterranean stock which had been established since a remote period in the area which they are found occupying in historical times. Basically, therefore, Dionysius of Halicarnassus was right.

But further consideration shows that this critical position is less solidly established than it looks. A great many features of Etruscan civilisation do in fact resemble certain aspects of particular civilisations in Asia Minor.

Considered separately, of course, none of these similarities would be decisive; but taken together they do weigh heavily in the balance. Excavations by French archaeologists in 1885 at Kaminia on the island of Lemnos at last yielded an inscription in a language related to Etruscan, the first to be discovered and still the only one of any importance. Later a few small fragments of inscriptions in what looked like the same language were discovered elsewhere on Lemnos. The main text is inscribed on a stone funerary stele representing the head and shoulders of a warrior bearing a lance, which is dated to the 7th century B.C. It was an important, though not a decisive, piece of evidence in the argument about Etruscan origins; for it showed that a language akin to Etruscan was spoken on an island off the coasts of Asia Minor before the conquest of Lemnos by the Athenians under Themistocles. The fact can be explained by a number of different hypotheses. The likeliest is that it reflects the passage at Lemnos of Tyrrhenians coming from Anatolia at about the time of their departure for the western shores of Italy.

Similarly, many features in the social, religious and artistic life of the Etruscans, and many of their customs, beliefs and techniques have their parallels in the ancient Near East. The important part played by women in Etruscan society had already attracted the notice of the ancients, and is confirmed both by the inscriptions which give the name of a man's mother as well as his father, and by the archaeological evidence which represents the wife, in death as in life, sitting or lying beside her husband in an attitude of familiar equality. Customs like these remind us of the matriarchal societies of the East, though in a less extreme form. This is what Herodotus has to tell us about the customs of the Lycians, a small people of Asia Minor:

"They take the mother's and not the father's name. Ask a Lycian who he is, and he answers by giving his own name, that of his mother, and so on in the female line. Moreover, if a free woman marry a man who is a slave, their children are full citizens; but if a free man marry a foreign woman, or live with a concubine, even though he be the first person in the State, the children forfeit all the rights of citizenship."

In the same way, the written sources and the evidence of painting and sculpture agree in showing the distinctive characteristics of Etruscan religion and its difference from the religions of Greece and Rome. The Etruscans were always noted for their anxious dependence on the gods and for their constant concern to penetrate the secrets of the future by means of the skilled interpretation of the divine signs which were regularly made manifest on earth. They had no sense of human freedom—a sense which the Romans, respectful though they were of the established rites, so successfully developed. They were, however, past masters in the study of thunder and the livers of sacrificial victims, in which they believed they could read the will of the gods with complete certainty. In 1877 a surprising bronze object was discovered near Piacenza: a representation of a sheep's liver, divided by lines incised on the surface into a large number of separate compartments. Within each of these compartments was inscribed the name of the god who, as it were, resided there, and who made known his decrees by the aspect of his particular part of the sacrificial organ. The reasoning here is quite complex. In the animal which is consecrated and offered to the gods, the liver, the seat and organ of life, is seen as a reflection of the world at the time of the sacrifice. On its surface are seen the mansions of the gods and, by a mysterious cosmic correspondence, these are also found in the sky above. The Piacenza liver is thus a microcosm of the larger world.

We know that the reading of the future from the livers of sacrificial victims was a constant preoccupation of the Etruscans; and again, it is only in the East that we find a close parallel to their elaborate and distinctive doctrine. In Asia Minor, in Syria and in Babylonia recent excavations have led to the discovery of a large number of terracotta models representing the livers of sacrificial animals, inscribed with predictions based on the conformation of the particular organ. The origins of Etruscan haruspicy must be sought, therefore, in a technique found as early as the 2nd millennium B.C., which was handed on from generation to generation and from people to people.

In the field of art, curiously enough, the evidence is less clear and less convincing. This is because from its earliest beginnings Etruscan art was profoundly influenced by Greece, which was itself undergoing a period of Oriental influence in the 7th century. The Oriental features in Etruscan art can, therefore, often be attributed to a Greek intermediary; or, if this is difficult to accept in a particular case, to the continuous relations which Etruria maintained with the countries of the East during the early centuries of its existence. In this period, therefore, detailed research is needed, and our findings must be most carefully considered. But when we visit the monumental chamber tombs hewn from the hillsides of southern Etruria—at Norchia, Barbarano or Sovana, for example—we cannot but be reminded of the rock sepulchres of Asia Minor.

Thus in the present state of knowledge a migration from the East still seems very probable. But at what point in time did it take place? Here again there are differences of opinion. Until quite recently the early date attributed by Herodotus to the Tyrrhenians' arrival in Italy seemed impossible to accept. In Etruria as in many other parts of Italy, particularly in the plain of the Po, there was found until the 8th century a culture of the first Iron Age known as Villanovan which, as we have seen, was ignorant of the art of writing and, socially, was still at a pre-urban stage. The people of this culture lived in villages of huts and cremated their dead; and the remains were deposited in collective cemeteries, with no trace of the individuality attributed to the dead man in Etruscan times. It was the general opinion, therefore, that the Villanovans represented an Italic people who had come into the Italian peninsula from the north or the east at the end of the 2nd or the beginning of the 1st millennium B.C., and that the Etruscan migration could only have taken place at the end of the 8th century, at about the same time as the first Greek colonists were beginning to settle on the coasts of southern Italy and Sicily. This meant that the Greek-Etruscan rivalry which was historically so well attested for later periods had begun with the first settlements of these peoples on the soil of Italy.

Some archaeologists, however—followed by some historians—have been impressed by material which has for some time been becoming available from excavations of protohistoric sites in Italy. It now appears that imports from the eastern Mediterranean do not—as was generally thought until recently—begin about the 8th century B.C., with the arrival of the first Greek colonists in Campania. At many places in southern Italy and Sicily excavation has revealed numerous fragments of Mycenaean pottery dated between 1400 and 1200 B.C. In the heart of Etruscan territory, at Luni, near San Giovenale, the latest excavations by the Swedish School at Rome have yielded a few scraps of this pottery. Finally, in the opinion of some scholars—though this is not generally accepted—the Mycenaean tablets, which have now been deciphered as a result of Ventris' and Chadwick's achievement in reading Linear B, appear to indicate the existence of continuous relations in the third quarter of the 2nd millennium B.C. between the Mycenaean kingdom of Pylos and Italy, in particular the Tyrrhenian coast to the north of Latium. Thus we may now legitimately ask—following in the footsteps of the late J. Bérard, who was the pioneer in this type of investigation—whether the Greek and Roman legends about the arrival of the worship of Heracles on the banks of the Tiber, the establishment of Evander on the Palatine, and the Trojan colonisation of Rome after the Trojan War (i.e. in the 13th century B.C.) might not be traced back to the appearance of Mycenaean seamen in the centre of Italy. At any rate the question remains open. Clearly, too, the new facts must make us look with fresh interest at Herodotus's story, which assigns to the same period the arrival in Etruria of emigrants from Lydia.

But one difficulty immediately springs to mind: can the Etruscans really have arrived in the 13th century, when there is no archaeological evidence of their civilisation, with its specific characteristics, until nearly five hundred years later, about the year 700 B.C.? How is such an enormous archaeological hiatus to be explained? To this powerful objection an answer has been suggested, which if it were right would be conclusive: that in fact during the centuries in question Etruria was not a cultural vacuum. There was a culture during this period, attested by finds in many cemeteries—that of the Villanovans. Moreover, it is suggested, the accepted theory that the Villanovans were an Italic people on whom the Etruscans superimposed themselves is not by any means so firmly established as it looks. At the end of the Villanovan period Oriental influences are already clearly evident; and—still more significantly—no real cultural hiatus can be observed between the end of the Villanovan and the beginning of the Etruscan period: the one passes insensibly into the other. The absence of any clean break means also that we must abandon the theory of the arrival of a new people: the Villanovans, in other words, were Proto-Etruscans. Thus if a people from the East did arrive in Etruria by sea this must have been at the beginning and not the end of the Villanovan period; that is, at the end of the 2nd millennium B.C. We thus come astonishingly close to Herodotus's story and to the dating it implies.

This view, put forward within the last few years, has received support from scholars of great authority. It is based on observed archaeological fact, and in some respects is most persuasive. But whenever complex historical questions are in issue the historical interpretation of the archaeological data is possible only with the help and support of other disciplines such as linguistics and the history of religions. Religious and linguistic data are essential in any attempt to define the characteristics of particular peoples and possible relationships between them: archaeology by itself may lead us into error. It has been shown at many different periods and in many different places that civilisations may be transformed and new peoples appear without any sign of a break in the pattern of life. Invading peoples, far from their country of origin, maintain their language and religion but often adopt the tools and techniques they find in their new country. Thus if we were to judge only by archaeological data many migrations would remain unnoticed.

The absence of a break between the Villanovan and Etruscan periods does not, therefore, seem to me conclusive. The religious and funerary customs of the two cultures are different; and in the innumerable Villanovan tombs excavated not a single inscription has so far been discovered. The written texts begin with the 7th century. Finally, the situation in the Po valley is difficult to reconcile with the theory that the Villanovans were Proto-Etruscans; for here the Villanovan civilisation lingered on until about 500 B.C., the date when—according both to tradition and the archaeological evidence—the Etruscan armies crossed the Apennines and conquered part of the plain of the Po.

This, then, is the stage reached in the controversy about Etruscan origins. The theory of their Oriental origin continues to gain support; the question of date remains open. For my own part, in spite of the strong views expressed to the contrary, I am still inclined to believe that Greek and Etruscan settlers arrived on the soil of Italy at about the same time, in the course of the 8th century B.C. If there were earlier arrivals, they were probably only Mycenaean traders, whose appearance would be sufficient to explain the legends and myths of the Greeks, Etruscans and Romans about the arrival of heroes and gods in Italy.

The second great problem of Etruscology is the language, which in spite of the continuing efforts of scholars remains extremely obscure. Since archaeology can contribute only indirectly to the solution of this problem we shall do no more than set out briefly the main points.

People are often surprised that all the efforts of the experts are unable to decipher a language which was spoken in the heart of Italy right up to the beginning of the Roman Empire. This surprise is reasonable enough, parti-

49

50

51

52

54

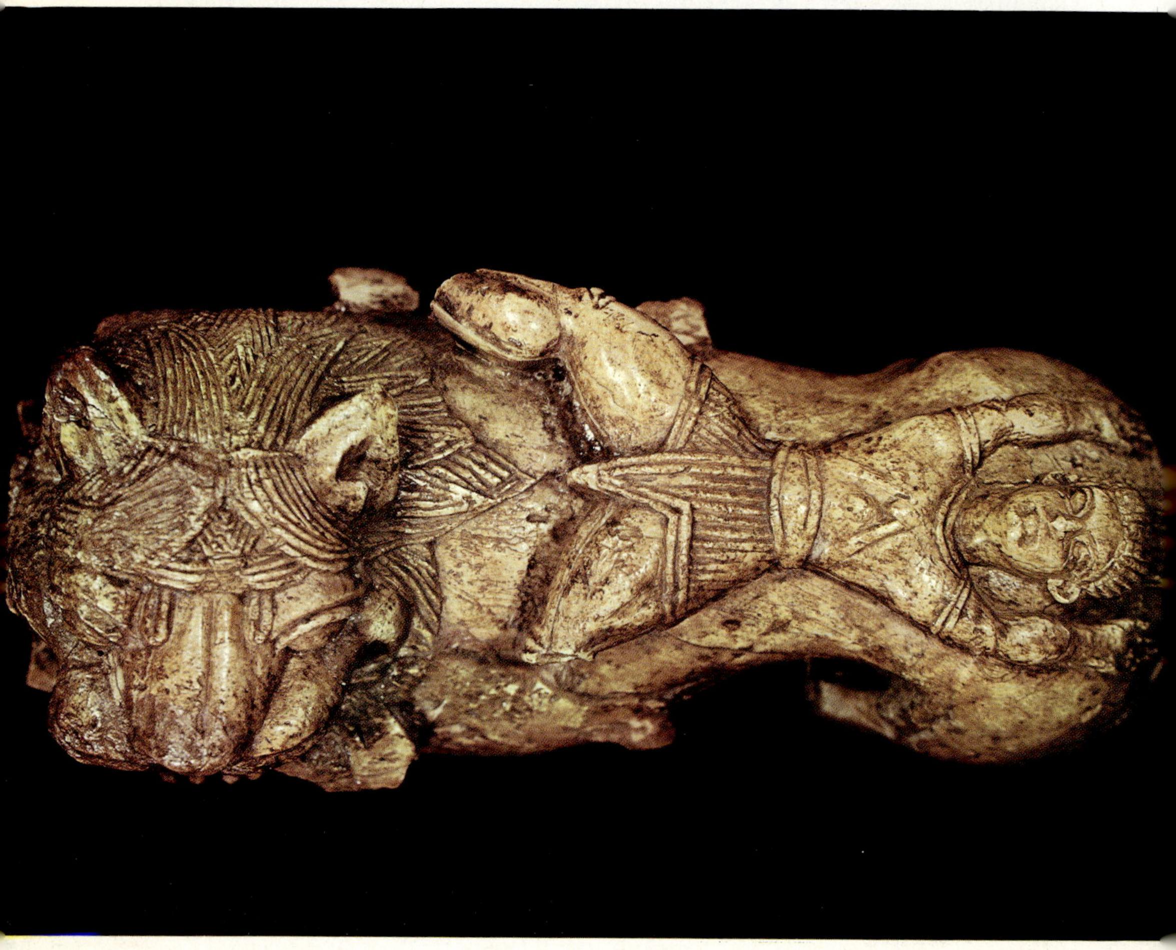

55

56

57

cularly among those who have little experience of the problems of language and linguistics. It is true that there have been many remarkable achievements in this direction since last century; but it is important to note what they involved. They concerned the decipherment of scripts which were themselves unknown but were used for writing languages which were already known or were related to known languages. The most famous instance is the French scholar Champollion, whose painstaking labours and profound learning enabled him to decipher the Egyptian hieroglyphics, which had hitherto remained incomprehensible in spite of the great quantity of inscriptions known. The discovery in 1799 of the famous Rosetta Stone had provided him and his fellow scholars with three versions of the same text—in hieroglyphics, in the demotic script, and in Greek. The text was a decree issued in 196 B.C. by a general synod of Egyptian priests in honour of King Ptolemy V Epiphanes. But the demotic script was also used to write a known language, Coptic, a modern form of Egyptian which was shown by the discovery to be derived from ancient Egyptian. Thus by going from the known (Coptic and Greek) to the unknown (Egyptian hieroglyphics transcribing a language from which Coptic was derived) Champollion succeeded in deciphering the hieroglyphics, and thus made possible the whole later development of modern Egyptology. Similar examples might be given of the decipherment of languages written in cuneiform script.

With Etruscan, however, the problem is quite different. The unknown element here is not the script: the Etruscan alphabet was borrowed from Greek, and it has been possible since the time of the Renaissance to read with reasonable accuracy the Etruscan texts which have been coming to light since ancient times, as a result either of chance discovery or of organised excavation. So far we have something like 10,000 texts—most of them, unfortunately, very short. Our difficulty is not, therefore, the reading of the script, nor the nature or number of the sources: it lies in the very nature of the language, which, apart from the hundred or so words known to us, remains completely obscure. There are only two ways of understanding a language whose nature and structure are unknown. One is through its relationship with a language or languages which are already known; the other is with the help of some external key—a bilingual dictionary, inscription or other document which contains a text both in the unknown language and in a language which is understood. In the case of Etruscan neither of these conditions is satisfied.

So far—and it seems unlikely that there will be any change in this respect—the linguists have been unable to discover any language or dialect which shows any relationship to Etruscan. Etruscan must have been in ancient times, as Basque is today, the surviving remnant of an old Mediterranean language, all other languages related to it having disappeared from the memory and the knowledge of men. We need some external aid to translation, and so far none has been found. It is hardly surprising, therefore, that Etruscan remains untranslatable. Consider again the case of Basque, also linguistically isolated and spoken by a people of some millions. If the Basque nation were to disappear—as fortunately it is unlikely to do—taking with it all the dictionaries, grammars and bilingual French-Basque texts, we should be in the same position in relation to Basque as we now are in relation to Etruscan: we should be able to read the language with ease, but not to understand it.

By what means, then, can we hope to make further progress? The answer must be—through archaeological discovery. Only this can provide us with bilingual texts of sufficient length, which will at last enable us to translate the texts which are now obscure to us; for there is little likelihood that we shall ever discover, buried in a distant library or remote monastery, the remains of some ancient manual on Etruscan, such as the Emperor Claudius himself compiled. And any such bilingual text would have to be of reasonable length and contain versions of the material—in Etruscan on the one hand and in Greek, Latin or perhaps Umbrian on the other—which were truly parallel.

One very recent discovery, of very great importance from the historical and religious points of view, raised hopes also in the linguistic field. It has already been briefly referred to. In July 1964 three Etruscan inscriptions *(Plates 51, 52)*, the longer of which contained 16 lines of text, and one Punic inscription *(Plate 53)*—all engraved on sheets of gold apart from one which was on a sheet of bronze—were discovered in the course of excavations which had been in progress for some years, under the direction of Massimo Pallottino, on the site of an Etruscan sanctuary at Pyrgi (Santa Severa), one of the ports of ancient Caere. In 1957 the chance discovery of some architectural terracottas had led the Institute of Etruscology of the University of Rome to begin the excavation of a sacred area, which was soon shown to be the famous sanctuary of Pyrgi mentioned in several ancient sources. According to some authors it was dedicated to the Greek goddess Eileithyia, according to others to Leucothea; but these Greek names must certainly have been applied to an Etruscan goddess. It was known also that Dionysius of Syracuse sacked the temple in 384 B.C. in the course of a daring attack on the very shores of Etruria.

The foundations of two temples standing close to one another were soon revealed; one had three *cellae*, the other only one. Many architectural terracottas dating from the first quarter of the 5th century B.C. were discovered, along with an inscription to Uni, the Etruscan Juno, which suggested that this was the goddess worshipped in the sanctuary.

During the summer of 1964 a stone basin filled with waste material was discovered in the space between the two temples. The material included several architectural terracottas and—less than 2 feet below the surface—the precious inscriptions, engraved on sheets of gold of almost exactly the same size and on one sheet of bronze. With the exception of the one on bronze, the inscriptions are perfectly preserved and reading them presents no problems. One of them can be understood in its entirety, in spite of certain difficulties with one or two words. It is written in the Phoenician language —very probably in Carthaginian—and is a dedication by the Etruscan ruler of Caere, Tiberie Belanas, to the goddess Astarte. The nature of the offering is given and its date, followed by the reason for the dedication—though here the Semitic scholars do not agree on the interpretation—and a second date; and there is a final formula referring to the statue of the goddess in the temple. The document itself, like the inscriptions, seems to date from about 500 B.C.; this is established by the archaeological context in which the inscriptions were found and by their palaeographical and philological characteristics. The longer of the Etruscan inscriptions is similar in content, and therefore in text, to the Punic inscription. It contains the name of the same dedicator, here transcribed in the form Thefarie Velianas; the name of the same goddess, here called Uni-Astarte; and a similar indication of date. Although not constituting a bilingual text in the proper sense, the inscriptions are parallel to one another and their wording is very close. In spite of this the Etruscan text is still extremely difficult to follow, and there is some uncertainty about the meaning of almost every single word. Nevertheless the information we can glean from the dedications is of the greatest importance, and we shall have more to say about this aspect later. But it is some indication of the difficulties of attempting to explain any Etruscan texts that even in this case, where we know with certainty the general sense of the text, the details of the semantic structure remain impenetrably obscure.

Such are the difficulties and uncertainties that confront us. But they must not make us forget that many other fields of Etruscan civilisation are appearing in a new light as a result of the advance of knowledge. The remainder of this study will show the immense contribution which archaeology has made towards this advance. But it seems necessary at this point to stress the basic principles which historical research must apply if it is to make the fullest and most effective use of the new and fundamental material produced by archaeology.

In the field of ancient history the method of research is based essentially on the systematic confrontation of the story told by the written sources with the factual material provided by the auxiliary disciplines. Among these archaeology undoubtedly occupies a central place. It helps to establish a sufficiently precise chronological framework for the history of civilisation; it alone can reveal to us all those things that the ancients did not find it necessary to mention in their writings, or that have been swept away in the irreparable loss of the greater part of ancient literature. In a field like Etruscology, where the native sources are lacking or at least largely unusable, it is natural to turn to the classical sources, Greek and Roman. These give us a great deal of information, but often information which is tendentious and biased. The Etruscans had been the Greeks' competitors, and often their enemies; and the Romans could not forget that they had ruled over Rome. Thus both Greeks and Romans sought to decry their merits and emphasise their faults. We must, therefore, examine very carefully any references to the Etruscans in Greek or Roman writings.

At the same time the sciences auxiliary to history must be brought into play on the largest possible scale. The new material provided by archaeology has often changed the aspect of our problems and altered the historical perspective. But the historian must apply the results of other disciplines as well, particularly linguistics and the history of religions. Nothing defines a people or a civilisation more closely than its language and its religion. These are the most stable elements in any human group, the most accurate reflection of its basic features and its psychology. The wider the range of studies brought in to assist the historian, the more efficient and successful will be the comparative method which is characteristic of the historian of today.

METHODS OF PROSPECTING

III

The progress of archaeological research is not the monopoly of any single school, nor of any particular area: research takes different forms according to the problem to be studied or the territory to be explored. But in recent years Etruria has been an area of choice for the application of new methods of prospecting, excavation and preservation; and it is, therefore, quite natural to discuss these techniques as they have been applied in Etruscan territory. It must not be forgotten, however, that they are of general application—tools which are available to every field archaeologist.

The archaeologist necessarily divides his activities into three stages—before, during and after excavation. We shall consider them here in the same order.

The period of prospecting is perhaps the most exciting of the three; for it ends in the discovery which is the supreme reward for all the uncertainties and anxieties that have gone before. Within the necessarily restricted compass of this essay the emphasis will be on the techniques which aid the archaeologist in his quest. But it is essential to note at the outset the importance of the purely human factor—the qualities and the flair of the archaeologist himself, his ability to enter into a direct and intimate contact with the district he is exploring and with its inhabitants. His education and training, and his capacity for applying his knowledge to practical situations, are of prime importance. It is also, I think, difficult to overestimate the amount of information he can obtain, in an area like Tuscany with an ancient cultural tradition, from friendly talks with the local people. There is one thing that can be acquired in no other way, either by direct observation or by the use of the auxiliary techniques, and that is information about chance discoveries made in the past by a peasant ploughing his land or a shepherd watching his flocks. As a rule no visible trace now remains of such finds; but the memory of them lingers in the mind of the man who discovered them or was present at their discovery, or of friends or relations of the finder. If you can gain a peasant's confidence and friendship he will reveal secrets which he alone knows; he will take you to the precise spot where he found a particular object; and he will be able to give you an excellent description of the object itself. How many discoveries, from one end of Tuscany to the other, have been due to information of this kind coming to the ears of the archaeologist who could interpret it!

In archaeology as in war everything depends on information: only on the basis of accurate information can we take advantage of the opportunities offered by luck or by chance. And the element of luck or chance is no less important today than it ever was, as there are plenty of famous recent examples to show. Thus the sensational discovery of the Dead Sea scrolls was due to the wanderings of a goat-herd in pursuit of a lost goat, which led him into the now celebrated cave where the jars containing the scrolls written in Hebrew and Aramaic had been hidden two thousand years before. Similarly the recovery of the Etruscan and Punic inscriptions of Pyrgi resulted from the chance discovery of a few fragments of terracotta. To say this does not, of course, detract from the achievement of those who realised at once the significance of these casual discoveries and took steps to follow them up.

The rapid progress of science and technology in our day has provided the archaeologist with a whole range of valuable new research techniques; and we must consider what these are and what contribution they have made to the progress of archaeology in Etruscan territory. The first, and not the least important, is air photography. The first air photograph—a view of Paris from a balloon—dates back to 1858; the first archaeological use of air photography to the beginning of the present century. The two world wars led to rapid technical progress, and the number of books and articles on the various archaeological applications of air photography is now not far short of the thousand mark. There is no doubt of the immense value of air photography to archaeology; the reasons for this are well known and need be only briefly summarised.

61 →

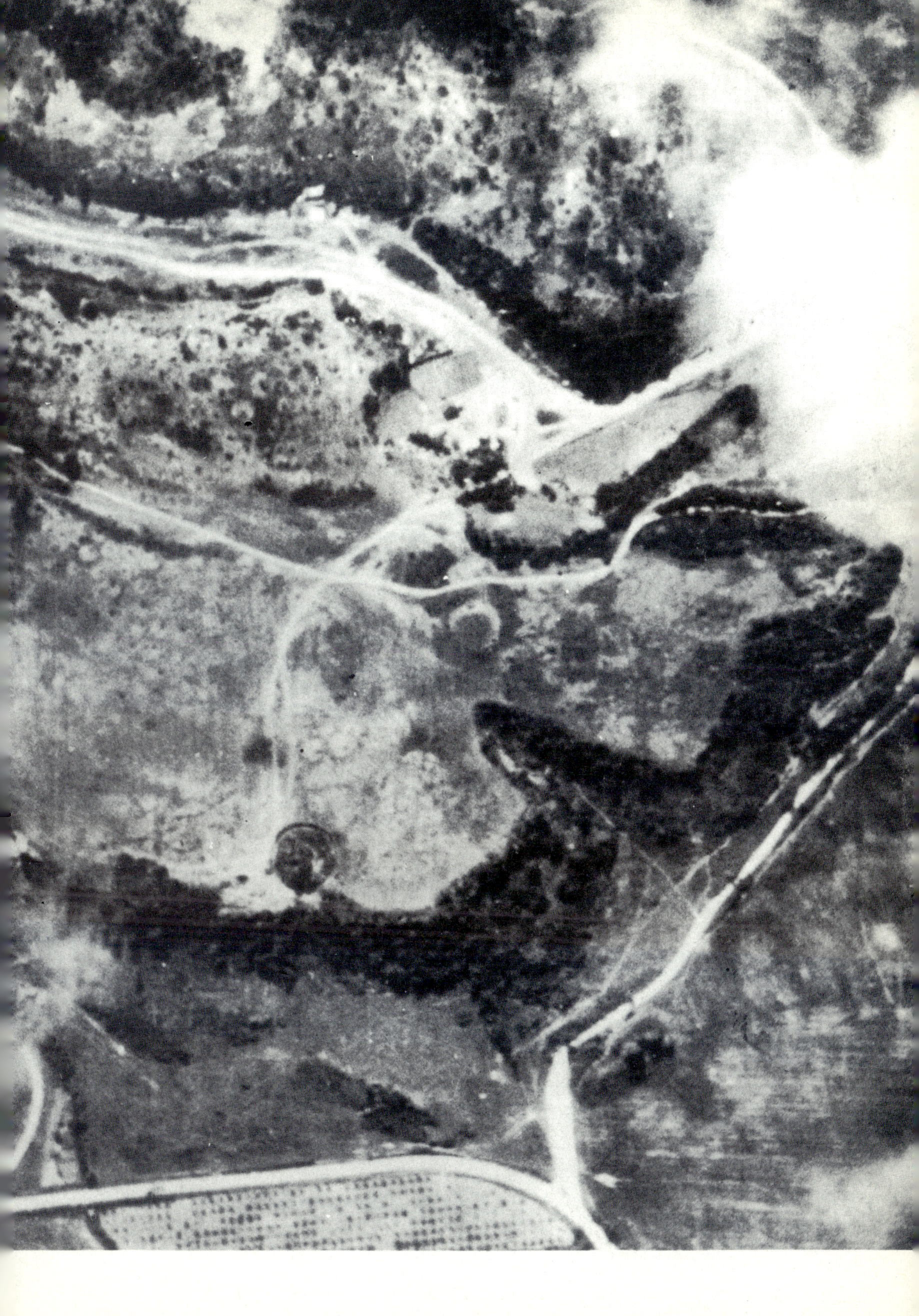

←65

67

68

69

71 - 72 →

70

73

74

75

80

81

84

85

←86

88

89

90

92,93 →

91

98 →

97

99 –

100

101

102

103

104

On an air photograph many details of the contours, the conformation of the soil, or the remains of ancient building are clearly shown, whereas to the naked eye they remain invisible or difficult to distinguish. The signs revealing an ancient occupation of the soil are of many kinds, but they have been usefully classified into three groups.

The first group consist of what are known as *shadow marks*. When the soil contains the remains of earthworks or walls, even if these cannot be seen distinctly on the ground, their shadows show up much more clearly on an air photograph taken either early in the morning or in the evening, when the shadows are longer in the rising or the setting sun.

A second series of data is provided by the so-called *crop marks*. When a well or a ditch has been dug, even at a very remote period, and later has been filled in, the greater depth of vegetable mould makes the crops grow higher and more thickly; and conversely the presence of wall foundations or ancient earthworks under the ground stunts the growth of grain and other plants and is shown in lighter lines on the photograph.

Finally, a third series of clues is provided by the colour of the soil. Earthworks or tumuli can often be detected on an air photograph even where they have been entirely levelled. This is because they were constructed with material dug from the earth which was not of the same colour as the surface of the surrounding soil. When the tumulus or earthwork was levelled to the ground the material would be scattered over a certain area, which would thus take on a new colouring. The difference is sometimes perceptible to the trained eye, but is much clearer on an air photograph. These are the so called *soil marks*.

In all fields of archaeology air photography has become an indispensable auxiliary to the prospector. In Etruria its achievements have been spectacular. One of the chapters in John Bradford's standard work, *Ancient*

Landscapes (London, 1957), is entitled "Etruria from the Air"; and the intensive surveys of Etruscan soil by the Milan engineer C. M. Lerici also started with coverage by air photography of the areas concerned. In this field, too, much valuable material has been contributed by General Schmiedt.

The first series of air photographs covering the Etruscan cemeteries go back as far as 1935; but more important were the photographs taken by the R.A.F. during the last war, which were systematically studied for the first time by John Bradford and published by him in 1947 in a preliminary article in *Antiquity*. Since then interest in the new technique has continued to increase, and a centre of air photography, the Aerofototeca, has been established at Rome with D. Adamesteanu as director. This has organised meetings and conferences and directed field work, and has already achieved important results.

The Etruscan cemeteries cover enormous areas—anything up to 1000 or 1200 acres, it may be, for the largest cemeteries like those of Cerveteri *(Plates 59–70)* or Tarquinia. In spite of incessant and indiscriminate digging by the clandestine operators who have been looting the cemeteries for the last century and a half, and the haphazard excavations of last century, there are still many areas awaiting a scientific survey, and many virgin tombs still to be discovered. Air photography has made it possible to establish the general layout of the great cemetery areas, for the tumuli which originally covered the tombs appear in the form of whitish patches standing out from the surrounding soil. Some of the older photographs taken by the R.A.F. and used by Bradford are impressive examples of the wealth of information which can be obtained with the help of the new technique. On a darker background of cultivated ground we see a scatter of white patches, the remains of the levelled tumuli. The arrangement and layout of the tombs are clearly shown, for cutting through the apparent confusion of the countless white circles we can follow the line of the great funeral roads, the *vie sepolcrali*, round which was organised and developed over the centuries the densely packed pattern of the tombs *(Plate 64)*.

Air photography is thus one of the essential elements in archaeological research, and in the particular field of Etruscology it has already great achievements to its credit. But there is a whole series of other recently developed techniques which must also be mentioned. It is hardly necessary to say that their development has not been due to archaeology, but to the necessities of research in the industrial field. Engineers prospecting for deposits of oil—or for that matter coal or other minerals, or concerned in general to analyse the structure of the subsoil—before undertaking major operations on the ground were able to call on the help of the geophysicists and the various research procedures they had developed. The point here is that the physical uniformity of the subsoil is modified by the existence of cavities, tombs or ditches—even where they have been filled in with earth—or by walls or other structures, just as it is by the presence of underground deposits of oil or veins of mineral ores. There are many different methods of discovering the places where the homogeneity of the soil is disturbed; but those which seem most likely to find a practical and effective application in archaeology are the methods based on the electrical conductivity of the ground.

The earth is a conductor of electricity, and in a particular area which is otherwise homogeneous this resistivity is modified by the presence of archaeological remains. From this came the idea of using in archaeological prospecting some very simple techniques which make it possible to detect such variations. The apparatus, a potentiometer *(Plate 71)*, is very easy to operate; and with its help, and a very small trained staff, it is possible to prepare resistivity maps for any desired area. First a line is selected in the area to be surveyed; then along this line, at regular intervals, electrodes are inserted, each of them separately wired to the apparatus; and finally the reading recorded by the potentiometer at each point is noted on graph paper, alongside a rough plan of the area covered. The same operation is then repeated over the whole survey area, and the result is a series of graphs which are quite easy to interpret. If a particular graph shows any unexpected irregularities this suggests the presence of underground remains which can be confirmed by test digging.

This method, which was used on a considerable scale for the purposes of industrial research from 1929-1930 onwards, was not applied to archaeology until just after the last war. In 1946 R. J. C. Atkinson, then of the University of Edinburgh, began to use it systematically in the survey of a Neolithic site at Dorchester, near Oxford, and obtained excellent results. Some ten years later C. M. Lerici, who had given up oil research to devote himself to archaeology, mainly in Etruscan territory, used the same method on a number of sites in Tuscany. The discoveries he made were so numerous and important that they not only enormously increased our stock of knowledge but in some places opened up entirely new possibilities for the future. The Etruscan cemeteries are, of course, an ideal field for this technique. The areas they occupy are known, and as a rule are free from modern building. Moreover the tombs themselves, being large cavities fairly near the surface (in general, perhaps, between 6 and 16 feet underground), are easy to find since they show up well on the resistivity curves. The systematic use of air photography and the resistivity survey, combined with a number of new methods of excavation to be referred to shortly, have revolutionised the whole technique of excavation in Etruria. This can be illustrated by a few figures taken from C. M. Lerici's publications.

In one of the cemeteries of Cerveteri, that of Monte Abbatone, perhaps ten new tombs had been found in the ten years before the application of the new methods; and then, in the course of a single campaign of ten months in 1956-1957, Lerici's team from the Polytechnic Institute of Milan identified 500 new tombs. Many of these, of course, had already been entered and despoiled of most of their contents, but in spite of this the campaign yielded some thousands of Etruscan, Italic and Greek objects which have enriched the resources of the Villa Giulia Museum. In 1958-1959 the same team tackled the necropolis of Tarquinia. Here no new painted tomb had been discovered for sixty-six years, the last one being the Tomb of the Bulls *(Plates 76–79)*, found in 1894. In eighteen months' work by the Lerici team a thousand new tombs were identified. These included, in 1958, a number of painted tombs of the first importance—the Tombs of the Olympiad, the Ship *(Plate 96)*, the Mouse, the Red Lions, the Jade Lions, and the Skull; and in 1959 three further painted tombs. Since then the pace of discovery has scarcely slackened; and indeed the mass of new finds is beginning to raise problems of study and of publication. We shall return to this point later. Already, however, we have a monumental publication by Sig. Moretti illustrating the newly discovered paintings, some of which are remarkably fine and of outstanding interest.

Another piece of apparatus contributed by the geophysicists is the electro-magnetic detector which is used to search for metal objects. It is sensitive to variations in the electro-magnetic field caused by the presence of metal in the subsoil, and was employed on a large scale for mine clearance in the last war. But its high sensitivity to the smallest scrap of metal has so far prevented it from being used systematically for archaeological research.

Another useful new instrument is the proton magnetometer *(Plate 72)*. It is interesting to note here that the only scientific attempt to explain the age-old mystery of the water diviner and his wand does so by reference to the surface variations in the electro-magnetic field which are found when there is water or metal in the subsoil. (See the book by Professor Y. Rocard of the Faculty of Science, Paris: *Le Signal du Sourcier*, Paris, 1963). For my part I am tempted to accept this explanation of a practice found in all ages and in all countries, which has often, though wrongly, been counted one of the occult sciences. The variation in the electro-magnetic field is felt by some people with particular force, and the forked wand which they hold at arm's length in a position of balance acts as a pointer to the signal they receive, their muscular contraction being converted into a movement of the wand. The mechanism of this physiological reaction has still to be explained; but I think it can already be said that the phenomenon of the water diviner has now received a rational explanation.

Many other recently developed prospecting techniques could be mentioned; but we are concerned in this book with Etruscology, and none of these methods has yet found an application in this field. Mention must, however, be made of under-water exploration, which has received a great impetus from the extraordinary popularity of under-water fishing off the Mediterranean coasts and the development of individual breathing apparatus which allows a man with a modicum of training to remain under water for a considerable period. With the help of this new apparatus divers have been setting out to look for archaeological remains, particularly of ancient vessels wrecked off the Mediterranean coasts of France and off the shores of Italy and Greece; and our knowledge of ancient shipping and of the sea trade routes of antiquity has benefited considerably as a result. There is scope for operations of this kind off the coast of Tuscany, and no doubt this will soon follow. And this method also has possibilities in the large lakes of Tuscany, inland seas like Lake Bolsena and Lake Trasimene, which must conceal many things of interest; for the Etruscans liked to live on their pleasant shores, using them for fishing and for easy communications with their neighbours.

The unprecedented increase in the pace of discovery in Etruria as a result of the new methods has led to the invention by the Lerici Institute of new auxiliary techniques designed to show whether a tomb is worth excavating before excavation begins. Many of the newly discovered tombs had already been completely rifled of their contents, either by excavations of earlier days or, more probably, by clandestine diggers—of whom there have always been many in the areas richest in tombs, and whose numbers have by no means declined in spite of the efforts of the authorities, for demand continues high on the antiquarian market. The figures published by C. M. Lerici are impressive. Of the total number of tombs discovered in the campaigns of 1956-1957 at Cerveteri and Tarquinia more than 98 per cent had already been violated, and 60 per cent had been completely emptied of their contents.

It would clearly avoid a good deal of wasted labour if the excavators knew what was in a tomb before they opened it; and some very ingenious devices have been invented for this purpose. Thus a new portable probe, controlled by an electric motor which is run off an easily transportable generating plant, enables a team of two operators to bore a hole some 4 inches in diameter through the soil above a tomb and through the ceiling of the tomb into the chamber itself. Through this hole is inserted a kind of periscope, simple in design but effective, which allows the archaeologists on the ground above to get a general view of the interior of the tomb *(Plate 73)*. If fuller information is required a metal cylinder of appropriate length is inserted into the tomb, bearing at its tip a small camera with a remote-controlled flash *(Plate 74)*. It is then a simple matter to take flash photographs of the whole inner surface of the tomb by gradually rotating the cylinder *(Plate 75)*. The photographs are printed quickly and give a good picture of the architectural characteristics of the tomb, the grave goods it contains, and the exact position of the entrance. These techniques have been remarkably successful in Etruria and have saved a great deal of valuable time. It can be seen, however, that they are applicable only to chamber tombs of the Etruscan type.

105

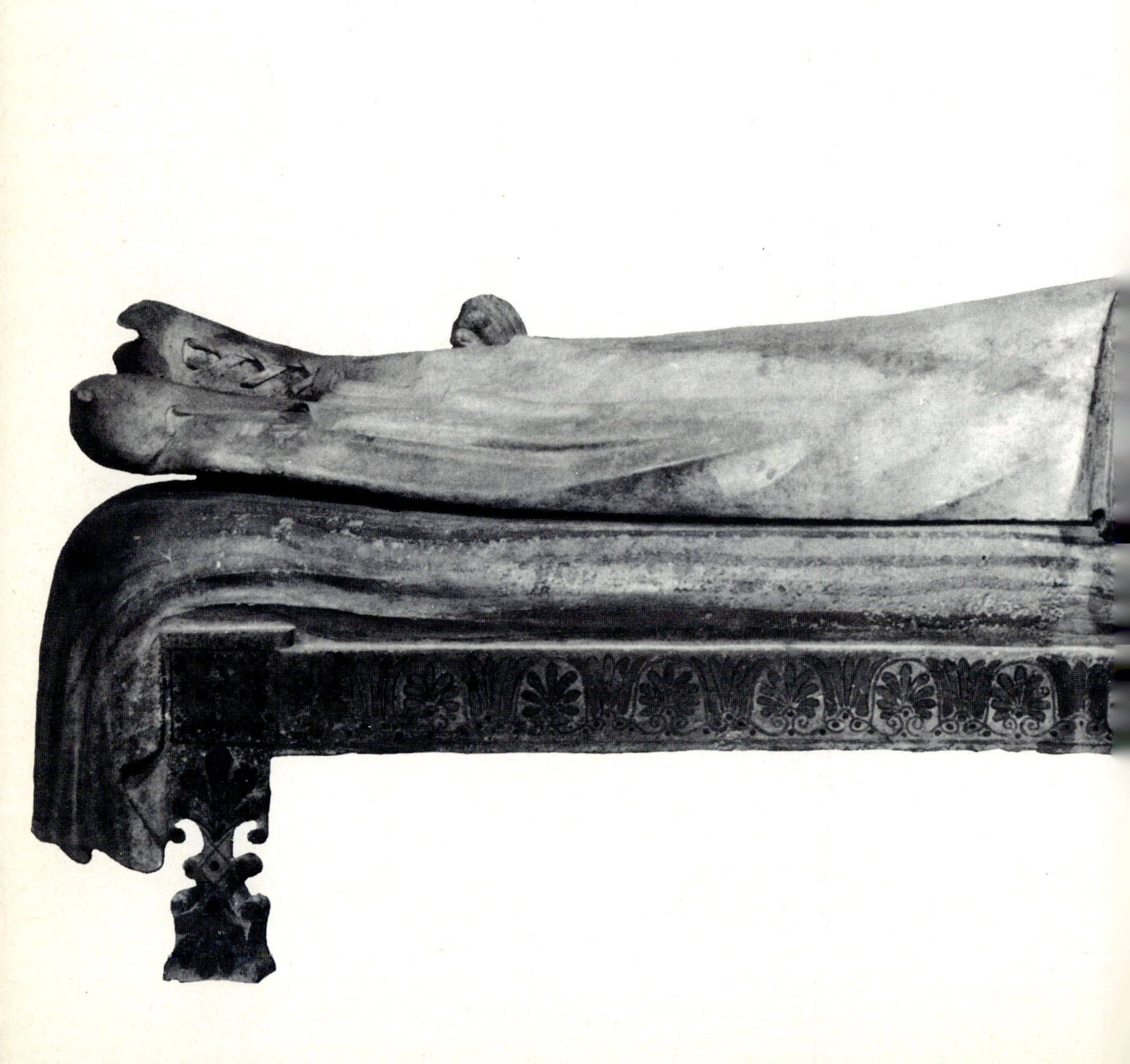

112

113

114

115

116

119

120

122

127 →

EXCAVATION EXAMINATION PRESERVATION

IV

It is unnecessary, in a study such as this, to discuss the general principles of excavation, which clearly are common to all archaeological work. Whatever the site to be explored the rules are the same, and they are absolutely binding on the archaeologist, who knows that in studying his evidence he must destroy most of it. The earth has opened its archives to him but he can only read them once. If he does a bad job it cannot be put right afterwards. He must, therefore, wring every drop of archaeological information from his site; he must neglect no trace of ancient occupation and must go right down to virgin soil. The stratigraphical method, distinguishing carefully each successive level, was developed by prehistorians, who had no other generally valid indication of relative dating: it is now the rule for all.

One or two comments may be made about the special features of excavation in Etruria and about the results already achieved or likely to be achieved. The unprecedented increase in the pace of field investigation in the cemetery areas as a result of the adoption of new techniques has brought with it the problem of finding enough trained archaeologists to carry on the work. In Italy, as in other countries, the number available is inadequate to the scale and urgency of the tasks. It is essential that additional teams of trained workers should be put into the field, for the work cannot wait. It is an error to believe that remains which have lain underground for two thousand years can be allowed to wait a little longer before being excavated: although the techniques of discovery have made sensational progress, the possibilities of rapid destruction have also increased alarmingly. The general public may be indifferent, but the danger is very real. The past, which has been preserved under its mantle of earth since prehistoric and ancient times, is now disappearing rapidly; and we shall have failed most lamentably in our duty to posterity if we merely look on at this destruction of our past and do nothing about it.

Everywhere the soil is being disturbed by great new building developments, the construction of roads and other engineering works, and above all by the use in agriculture of heavy tractors and new ploughing methods which cut deeply into the earth. In a country like Italy there has certainly been more destruction of archaeological material in the last twenty years than in all earlier centuries. Air photographs taken only a few years ago in different parts of Italy clearly show traces of settlements of the Neolithic and metal-using ages; in recent photographs there is not a sign of them. In Etruria itself the heavy tractors frequently crash through the ceilings of Etruscan tombs, causing irreparable damage. The Italian authorities, alarmed at this state of affairs, have taken certain protective measures. The only really effective step has been the acquisition by the State of archaeological areas of particular importance, which are thus protected for all time. But this is of course possible only in a limited number of special cases. Elsewhere the law requires that where antiquities are discovered in the course of any building or other operations this must be notified by the contractors to the local authority, who in turn inform the archaeological authorities (i.e., the regional Superintendency of Antiquities). These authorities, after examining the site, decide whether it is necessary to interrupt the contractors' operations and carry out a proper survey. Contractors, of course, dislike delays of this kind, which cost them money; and word seems to get round among the men on the site that it is better not to say too much about any chance discoveries they may make.

Mention must also be made of clandestine excavators, who are particularly active in Etruscan territory because of the relative ease of excavation of the tombs and the high prices which Greek or Etruscan works now fetch on the market. Clandestine digging, of course, has taken place in all ages; and in Etruria it is certainly not a new development. The new factor which increases the losses from unauthorised excavation is that the clandestine operators now have available to them all the techniques used by archaeologists.

Another disquieting feature is that while the size and value of the collections in museums continue to grow the arrangements for looking after them there are all too often totally out of date and inadequate. As a result valuable exhibits sometimes go missing, and Etruscan scholars in Italy have justifiably expressed alarm about such losses. Difficulties of this kind are not, of course, unknown in other countries than Italy; but there seems to be a general reluctance on the part of the authorities to find the money to pay for the extra staff our museums and art galleries need. As a result they sometimes cannot afford to remain open all day; and even the Louvre, besieged as it is by tourists from all over the world, has to close some of its rooms for two hours at lunch-time.

If we now pass from the Etruscan cemeteries—where excavation is fairly straightforward, provided it is carefully and scientifically conducted—to consider the sites of protohistoric or Etruscan settlements, the problem becomes more complex, but offers the prospect of a rich harvest of historical and chronological information. The pre-Etruscan and Etruscan periods in the history of Rome now appear in a new light as a result of the stratigraphical excavations carried out since the last war on various sites in archaic Rome, in the Forum and on the Palatine. We thus learn that Rome only became a city in the proper sense when Etruscan conquerors appeared on her soil and brought her into contact with a superior civilisation. This decisive event took place rather later than the tradition requires, about 575 B.C. It was at this stage that the villages of huts in the Forum disappeared and the Forum was paved for the first time—an indication of a move to unify the scattered settlements into a city.

But if archaeology has given us evidence about the beginning of the Etruscan kingship in Rome, bringing the date down a little later than the traditional one, it has also thrown fresh light on its end, when Rome reverted to the status—which she was for long to retain—of a quite modest Latin town living alongside a number of similar towns in the Alban Hills and the plain of Latium. The departure of the Tarquins following a "national revolution" led by Brutus is given much too early a date in the tradition. The architectural terracottas and Greek figured vases dating from the beginning of the 5th century B.C. which have been discovered on a number of sites in archaic Rome show that at least until about the year 470—or 450 according to some scholars—the material conditions of life in Rome do not change, and the city is apparently still prosperous. Signs of a decline in prosperity do not appear until after the first quarter of the 5th century. Then there is a falling off of imports from Greece, and the architectural terracottas disappear. The evidence in other fields points in the same direction: thus round about the traditional date of the expulsion of the Tarquins there is no break in religious life, and a number of new and important sanctuaries are founded. The break comes after 470 B.C.; and this is very probably the date when the Etruscan tyrants left Rome—though not because of an internal rising but probably in consequence of the heavy defeats which the Greeks inflicted at this time on the fleets of the Etruscans and their Carthaginian allies.

This important correction of the accepted dating was a considerable achievement, largely due to the progress of archaeological research in Rome; but it was still necessary to consider why the Roman annalists had found it necessary to put the departure of the Tarquins at least thirty years—and perhaps rather more—earlier than its actual date. Here again archaeology comes to our aid. The archaeological evidence shows that the temple of Jupiter Capitolinus, which was to become the religious centre of Rome and later of the whole Roman world, was indeed founded at the traditional date, the end of the 6th century B.C., and was built by the Etruscan kings, as the annalists were obliged regretfully to concede. The date assigned by the ancients to the dedication of the temple—509 B.C.—is certainly correct. In any case it would have been difficult to alter the date of an event of such importance, from which followed all the rest of the traditional story. But it was essential that this most important Roman temple should not appear to be a purely Etruscan creation: at least the dedication must be attributed to the Romans. There was only one way to achieve this: the departure of the Etruscans from Rome had to be advanced so that, almost miraculously, they left the soil of Rome a few months before the act of dedication, the glory of which could thus be attributed to a Roman consul. This is the interpretation I would give of this most famous and most dramatic of the stories told in the annals of Rome; and this is the source of the tale of the rape of Lucretia and the revolt led by Brutus. Hence the inaccurate but dramatic picture of the Romans ridding themselves of the Etruscan occupation, establishing a republic, and then marking the occasion by the dedication of their most famous temple.

Thus a great deal of light is being thrown on the history of Etruria by stratigraphical studies of Etruscan soil or of the sites of cities which were founded or temporarily occupied by the Etruscans. But the archaeologist's task does not end with his excavations: often, indeed, the main part of the work has still to come. The material he finds must be analysed and dated, it must be restored, it must be preserved and published; and these are all operations that require time, care, and a rigorously scientific approach.

We now have at our disposal a whole series of scientific methods for the analysis of archaeological material. The different photographic techniques have a particularly important part to play. Microphotography and macrophotography can reveal details invisible to the naked eye, and with their help great strides have recently been made in the study of the Etruscan techniques of gold jewellery, granulation and filigree. X-ray photography has a variety of uses: it allows an object to be examined in depth, and in the study of Etruscan wall paintings has enabled the preliminary drawings and sketches to be distinguished from the final painting, so that we can follow successive stages in the work of the ancient painters.

All these new methods of analysis offer us new means of distinguishing the counterfeits which are so common in the trade and sometimes even find their way into the great museums of Europe and America. There are probably more fakes in the field of Etruscan archaeology than in any other; and, as some recent examples have shown, Etruscan fakes have given rise to more violent controversy than any others. We shall refer briefly to one or two recent cases, and shall then consider why counterfeiting is particularly active in the field of Etruscan archaeology.

The British Museum for many years displayed as genuine an Etruscan sarcophagus in terracotta representing the reclining figures of a man and a woman. The sides of the caskets were decorated with bas-reliefs, and the whole thing was borne on four legs carved in the form of sphinxes. It resembled the famous sarcophagus, now in the Louvre, discovered at Cerveteri in 1850 by the Marchese Campana *(Plate 108)*, and the one found in the same cemetery at the end of the last century, which is one of the glories of the Villa Giulia Museum in Rome *(Plates 109, 110)*. The three sarcophagi have the same general structure, but on examination the one in the British Museum shows some peculiar features which betray modern workmanship. The feet of the funeral couch have no functional role, there is something awkward and untypical about the attitude of the man and woman, and the modelling of the faces accentuates the archaic features—long heads, sharp profiles, almond-shaped eyes—characteristic of Etruscan works produced under Ionian influence. Thus, stylistically, there is something exaggerated—hyper-Etruscan, if you like—about this work, which was for so long admired by the general public and indeed by scholars as well. About the year 1930 it was shown to be a fake, and it was later withdrawn from exhibition, though it is still one of the most interesting examples of the art of the faker as applied to Etruscan archaeology. The sarcophagus in the Louvre had been taken as the model, but its characteristics had been exaggerated and distorted. In order to give an appearance of genuineness to his work the counterfeiter had taken the trouble to paint an inscription on the lid of the sarcophagus; but it was copied from an inscription on a gold fibula from Chiusi, and to the experts this only confirmed the spuriousness of the piece.

Then there were the huge terracotta figures of warriors in the Metropolitan Museum of Art in New York. A scientific publication has recently provided final confirmation of the doubts which had long been felt about their genuineness. Chemical analysis and an examination of the circumstances in which they first appeared have shown that they are modern, as some experts had in fact suggested more than a quarter of a century ago. It must be said that these works were decidedly unusual, and it seems strange that so many scholars should have believed in their authenticity for so long. In fact they had been manufactured at the beginning of the First World War, in 1914, by some well known counterfeiters of Orvieto, the Riccardis, assisted on this occasion by one Fioravanti, since it was a long and delicate operation to produce these huge pieces. When the Metropolitan Museum of New York acquired them they were, very convincingly, in fragments, and it was not until 1933 that the figures were pieced together and put on show. Conceived and executed by skilled craftsmen, but at a time when the archaic terracotta statues of the school of Veii were not yet known (the Apollo was discovered only in 1916), they were very different in style from archaic Etruscan terracottas. They attracted great public interest, however, and when an Italian scholar, Massimo Pallottino, denounced the fraud in 1937 his voice went unheard. The massive figure of the warrior is merely a larger version of an archaic Greek bronze from Dodona, and the helmeted head is a variant of the first warrior's head. The other figure, with its body drawn out to exaggerated length, has a more Etruscan look about it, for it is imitated from Etruscan votive bronzes with similarly elongated bodies *(Plates 3–5)*. Spectrographic analysis showed that the terracotta was of recent origin; and the story was finally rounded off when it proved possible to trace one of the original counterfeiters, Alfredo Adolfo Fioravanti. (By this time the Riccardis themselves were dead). Fioravanti explained in 1961 how the warriors had been made, with his help, in the Riccardis' workshop in Orvieto and—among many other interesting details—confirmed that the model had been the famous bronze from Dodona, taken from a reproduction in an illustrated book. The whole episode is a most instructive case study in the launching, acceptance, and final exposure of a fake.

And this is not by any means the end of the story of Etruscan counterfeits. A terracotta statue in the Etruscan style representing Diana and her hind was considered in Rome to be a fake and was exported in the ordinary course of trade to Switzerland. It was then acquired, some years ago, for the Museum of St Louis in the United States, where it was exhibited as genuine. A competent scholar who is now dead, R. Herbig, discussed it in a detailed publication as a genuine Etruscan work. And yet, as most experts now recognise, it is a modern version of a type of archaic Etruscan statue. The face follows the archaic type, with its slanting eyes, pointed chin and characteristic smile; but we feel a modern hand in the execution.

In these cases even the experts were led astray; but there can be no room for similar doubt in the countless small objects—"Etruscan" bronzes, mirrors and jewels—which make up the main output of the counterfeiter's art. These are either merely copies of well known pieces or imitations of poor quality in which the stylistic anachronisms are easy to detect. There has been an extraordinary proliferation in the last few decades of Etruscan fakes of all kinds; and the reasons for this are not far to seek. In the first place there has been the great vogue for Etruscan art—demonstrated, for example, by the size of the crowds who flocked to see the great exhibition of Etruscan art at Milan and Paris in 1955. Then there has been the popularity of Etruria among visitors and tourists. The collector's instinct leads the visitor to try to pick up some Etruscan find on the spot, and he flatters himself that he knows a "good" vase or jewel when he sees one. It is a curious psychological phenomenon that even an intelligent man regards archaeology as a subject anyone can understand. And this fundamental error is sometimes compounded by the visitor's desire to make a good buy—his naive conviction that he can get a valuable object at a bargain price. As a result foreign tourists and diplomats in Rome provide a ready market for the output of an army of small fakers, who consequently are able to drive a thriving trade.

To these psychological motives must, I think, be added a factor inherent in the objects themselves rather than in those who buy them. Etruscan art shows great diversity at different times and places. It contains a variety of opposing trends, a refined and disciplined style which faithfully follows Greek models and a more local and popular style which abandons Hellenism and gives free play to imagination, improvisation, and a direct and straightforward view of life. What a difference there is between a splendid jewel of the archaic period, vying in perfection of decoration and technique with the most refined products of Greek workshops, and a modest and spirited local terracotta representing, rather clumsily, a god or his worshipper! A peripheral art like that of Etruria, modelled on Greek art but lagging behind it and developing in a number of different directions, is a particularly promising field for counterfeiters; a dangerous one for the amateur and a difficult one even for the expert. We find another example of the same thing in the Greco-Scythian art which was produced in Greek workshops on the shores of the Black Sea. One characteristic product of this art was jewellery of Greek type but of exceptionally large size, which has certain very distinctive features. Although the artists were Greek the spirit of these pieces was not: they were designed for barbarian princes with a taste for luxury, ostentation and display. Taking advantage of the divergence between Greek jewellery and this Greco-Scythian work, the fakers have managed to deceive the public, and sometimes even the experts, with their skilful imitations. Some of their work is famous, like the Tiara of Saitapharnes which was one of the show pieces of the Louvre until it was recognised as a skilful forgery.

Thus the techniques of analysis and examination worked out in the laboratory make a decisive contribution to our understanding of the material discovered by excavation, and the same techniques have enabled us to show that certain works wrongly thought to be Etruscan were in fact modern. Other methods developed by the physical and chemical sciences are no less valuable in the preservation or restoration of the finds, the older ones as well as the latest ones. In the field of Etruscology there is an important and sometimes an urgent task to be done in this direction.

Like all ancient bronzes, Etruscan bronzes need to be cleaned, protected and cared for when they are affected by the condition known as bronze disease. But precautions of this kind, which apply to all excavated material, are especially urgent in the case of works which are particularly exposed to a progressive process of destruction, like the frescoes in the Etruscan tombs. Unfortunately, the frescoes in the painted tombs of Tarquinia *(Plates 76–104)*, Orvieto and Chiusi, which form an important part of our artistic heritage, are deteriorating very rapidly. Some paintings which were fresh and well preserved when they were found are now either lost for good or on the point of disappearing. Once the tomb has been opened the variations in temperature and humidity in the underground chamber are a source of danger to the wall paintings, and they have also suffered damage at the hands of the large numbers of visitors entering them without proper supervision, and from the pollution of the air caused by the smoky torches of the guides. Worse still, clandestine excavators managed not long ago to steal some newly discovered frescoes at Tarquinia by skilfully detaching them from the walls of the tomb. Steps must be taken to put an end to losses of this kind.

In order to save the paintings which had been damaged by natural causes the Italian experts took a decision which was heroic as well as wise. Using the latest techniques, representatives of the Institute of Restoration in Rome—a well equipped establishment which ought to have its equivalent in other countries—detached the frescoes from the rock face, fixed them on canvas, and then removed them to museums where they could be properly looked after. It was a delicate operation, for the frescoes were painted on a very thin layer of plaster, not more than a centimetre thick, and sometimes directly on the rock. In every case, however, it was completely successful, and it has been possible in this way to reconstitute in the museums some of the painted tombs which are among the treasures of Etruria *(Plates 95–99)*.

But this procedure requires money and skilled staff, and it has been possible to apply it only in a limited number of cases. The very great majority of Etruscan paintings are, therefore, still underground in the huge cemeteries of Tarquinia, and it is essential that steps should be taken to ensure their survival. We have recently had the example of the hazards to which the splendid prehistoric cave paintings of Lascaux were exposed, and it has been necessary to resort to the regrettable expedient of closing them to the public for an indefinite period in order to prevent their total ruin. In archaeology as in other fields prevention is better than cure, and it is certainly much better to anticipate the danger than to have to adopt radical measures to make good the damage after it has occurred.

As excavation continues and the scale of discovery increases, so the problems of the museums and the need for reorganisation become more urgent. These are general problems, but they are felt with particular acuteness in the field of Etruscology, where the pace of exploration has been steadily increasing in recent years. The principles of museum organisation have been completely reviewed, and though general agreement has not yet been reached there has been a fairly general move towards rational solutions. In the past a museum was merely a place for the preservation of all the material produced by excavation, and everything was crammed into display cases which, it must be admitted, were not calculated to interest the ordinary visitor. Nowadays—and rightly—the tendency is to make the displays less crowded and more selective, and to keep the bulk of the archaeological material which is of interest to the specialist in well lighted and easily accessible galleries and store-rooms. In the field of Etruscology there is a striking contrast between the Vatican Museum, which has retained the atmosphere and arrangement of past centuries, and the Villa Giulia Museum, which has been boldly and successfully fitted into the handsome and historic palace of Pope Julius II, and whose up-to-date conception and layout make it most attractive to the visitor.

In the field of museum practice there are still many difficult problems to be solved. If we are to solve them we must have a clear understanding of the proper purpose of an archaeological museum; we must attempt to achieve rational solutions to the problems which confront us; and we must seek to make it possible for the public as a whole to share in the heritage which has come down to them from the past.

CONCLUSION

At the end of this study we can appreciate both the promising future which lies ahead of archaeology in Etruria and the dangers to which it is exposed. As the discoveries made in the last ten years show, the possibilities are enormous. The material available to us has increased considerably, and archaeological research has been equipped with a variety of new resources which open up the way to further development. And it is clear that the possibility of advance in our linguistic and historical knowledge depends on the progress of archaeology. We cannot hope to get out of the dead end we have reached in the study of the Etruscan language unless the material available for study is increased by the discovery of new written texts. But it is fair to say that our hopes of important discoveries of this kind are not entirely illusory. We must remember that the exploration of urban sites has only begun in recent years, and we may reasonably hope to find on these sites religious or legal inscriptions written both in Etruscan and in a known language.

An example will show the wealth of information we can draw from new Etruscan texts, even though we cannot in the present state of knowledge grasp more than their general sense. Mention was made in an earlier chapter of the recent discovery at the sanctuary of the port of Pyrgi of one Punic and three Etruscan inscriptions written on sheets of gold and bronze. These give us direct evidence of the relationship established in the archaic period between deities worshipped by very different peoples, and provide the first intimation of a connection which Virgil was to recall five centuries later at the beginning of the *Aeneid.* The Greeks gave the name of Leucothea or Eileithyia to the goddess worshipped in the sanctuary of Pyrgi; and the inscriptions discovered in 1964 show that in fact the Etruscan goddess Uni and the Phoenician Astarte were worshipped there. This of course raises the question of possible links between these different goddesses.

The temple must undoubtedly have been dedicated to Uni, the patron of many Etruscan cities, who corresponded in functions, characteristics and name to the Italic and Roman Juno. Uni-Juno is the goddess of married women, the goddess of fruitfulness who protects women and assists them in childbirth. But she can also have a warlike aspect, like the Juno Quiritis of Falerii who bears a lance or the Juno Caprotina of Lanuvium who carries a kind of *aegis*. We might have expected the Greeks, who knew Caere well (and were indeed supposed to have brought Greek culture to it), to make the natural identification of the Etruscan goddess with their goddess Hera, the protector of wives and granter of fruitfulness, whose importance in the archaic period is shown by so many inscriptions. They do in fact speak of Eileithyia, the daughter of Hera, who presides at childbirth, and also of Leucothea, the white goddess of the sea; and here there is no connection with the original model, for in Greek mythology Leucothea is the unfortunate Ino who brought up the young Dionysus and was struck with madness by Hera, and who killed her own children and was transformed into a Nereid. What can give rise to interpretations of this kind? All the various suggested explanations have proved unsatisfactory. It now seems to me likely, however, that the original interpretation put forward by the ancients was not Greek but Latin. Uni was called by the Romans Juno Lucina or Mater Matuta, two very closely related matron goddesses. But the *interpretatio graeca* of Juno Lucina was Eileithyia, and of Mater Matuta Leucothea: hence the names used in the Greek sources which have come down to us. The case for this suggestion is argued in the *Comptes Rendus de l'Académie des Inscriptions et Belles Lettres*, 1968. And it is quite natural in this religious context to find the goddess Astarte, an accepted and powerful deity, recognised by the Etruscan ruler of the time—about 500 B.C.—as being the same patron goddess as Uni herself. Astarte was the great Phoenician goddess who was worshipped at Carthage in the archaic period and later gave place to Tanit. The identification with Juno remains constant.

Thus we find at Caere, in the year 500 B.C., the situation reflected in the opening lines of the most famous Latin poem, the *Aeneid*. "Formerly," writes Virgil, "a city occupied by settlers from Tyre—Carthage—watched from afar Italy and the mouth of the Tiber. Rich it was, and fiercely devoted to war. It is said that Juno preferred it to any other place, even to Samos. *There* were her arms; *there* was her chariot." A little later on we hear how, in the heart of the new city of Carthage, "Dido of Sidon built a great temple to Juno, no less considerable by the offerings made by men than by the power of the goddess..." Thus the destiny of Carthage is protected by a warlike Juno; but it is also, and at the same time, under the protection of the Semitic goddess Astarte-Tanit. The close connection between Uni-Juno and Astarte which the Pyrgi inscriptions attest in the archaic period was still familiar to Virgil, and these inscriptions found so recently in an Etruscan port prove the correctness of the religious and historical reconstructions of the greatest of the Roman poets.

Thus the prospects held out by archaeology in the field of Etruscan studies are wide and promising. But the dangers, as we have seen, are also great and pressing. The remains of the past buried in the soil of Tuscany—and indeed in all the countries of the West—have never before been in such danger of disappearing for ever without becoming known. We cannot look on indifferently at the destruction of our past, which seems so near to sinking into final oblivion. The continually increasing pace of development of our towns and countryside, combined with the new methods of ploughing, is creating a situation fraught with peril for archaeology, and it is time that the danger was generally appreciated. There has been more destruction—as we have already noted and must repeat again—in the last twenty years than in all earlier centuries. A number of scholars, realising the situation, have already raised the alarm about the danger to the artistic heritage of Tuscany and of Italy in general. There is a need for similar warnings in other countries as well, where remains of the past are disappearing ever more frequently. The march of progress offers benefits to man, but we must also clearly realise the dangers which it brings with it. Only this realisation can prevent disaster; a disaster for which we should bear the full responsibility.

SUGGESTIONS FOR FURTHER READING

R. BLOCH, "Où en est la technique archéologique?", in *Annales, économies, sociétés, civilisations*, July-September 1952.

M. PALLOTTINO, *The Meaning of Archaeology*, Thames and Hudson, London, 1968.

C.M. LERICI, *Alla scoperta delle civiltà sepolte*, Milan, 1960.

M. PALLOTTINO, "Il problema delle falsificazioni d'arte etrusca di fronte alla critica", in *Atti dell'Accademia nazionale di San Luca*, Rome, 1961.

D. von BOTHMER and Joseph NOBLE, *An inquiry into the forgery of the Etruscan warriors in the Metropolitan Museum of Art*, in *Metropolitan Museum of Art Papers*, No. 11, 1961.

R. BLOCH, *Etruscan Art*, Thames and Hudson, London, 1959.

M. MORETTI, *Nuovi monumenti della pittura etrusca*, Milan, 1966.

J. HEURGON, *Daily Life of the Etruscans*, London, 1964.

Ulisse (Florence), issue for April 1966.

R. BLOCH, *Tite Live et les premiers siècles de Rome*, Editions des Belles Lettres, Paris, 1965.

CHRONOLOGY OF ETRUSCAN CIVILISATION

I – The Origins

Second half of 2nd millennium B.C.	Contact between the Italic populations of Sicily and southern and central Italy and the Greek civilisation of the Mycenaean period.
13th century B.C.	Legendary migration of Lydians, led by Tyrrhenus, to the coasts of Tuscany: the supposed ancestors of the Etruscan people.
9th–8th centuries B.C.	Italic Iron Age civilisation, the Villanovans, in Tuscany and certain other parts of Italy. In the Po valley the Villanovan civilisation flourishes until about 500 B.C.

II – 7th and 6th Centuries: the Development and Apogee of Etruscan Civilisation

First half of 7th century	Establishment and rapid growth of Etruscan cities on the southern and northern coasts of Tuscany. Development of Greek towns founded from the mid 8th century onwards on the south coasts of Italy and Sicily. The early years of Rome (founded 753) are a period of slow and peaceful development.
7th century	Large orientalising tombs of Caere (Regolini-Galassi) and Praeneste (Barberini and Bernardini). Orientalising style in Etruscan art. Magnificent jewellery and ivories. Maritime power of the Etruscans, competing with the naval forces of Carthage, their ally, and Greece, frequently their enemy.

6th century	The Etruscans, in alliance with Carthage, command the Western Mediterranean. Extension of Etruscan power into Campania.
Second half of 6th century	Extension of Etruscan power into the Po valley, where Villanovan civilisation (Arnoaldi phase) gives place to Etruscan civilisation (the Certosa culture). Foundation of Marzabotto, Felsina, Spina, Adria. Development of Padan Etruria.
535	Etruscan naval victory over the Phocaeans off Aleria (Corsica).
524	Etruscan defeat by a Cumaean army led by Aristodemus.
Second half of 6th century to early 5th century	Splendour of archaic art — first Ionian and later Attic in style. Tomb paintings of Tarquinia; painted plaques of Caere — Campana (Louvre) and Boccanera (British Museum). Bronzes of Vulci and other towns. Large terracotta sarcophagi of Caere (Louvre and Villa Giulia, Rome). Painted terracotta antefixes. Terracotta group from the Temple of Apollo at Veii, the only work by an Etruscan artist whose name is known (Vulca).

III – 5th Century: the Decline of the Etruscan Empire Begins

Beginning of 5th century	Difficulties in Latium.
509	Expulsion of the Tarquins from Rome. Campaign by Porsenna, king of Clusium, and capture of Rome.

504	Aristodemus of Cumae and the Latins defeat a son of Porsenna at Aricia, near Rome.
499	Rome defeats the Latins at Lake Regillus.
474	Defeat of the Etruscans by the Syracusans in a naval battle off Cumae. Beginning of the decline of Etruscan naval power.
First half of 5th century	Painted tombs of Tarquinia. Small bronzes; bronze braziers, candelabras and tripods.
Second half of 5th century	Disintegration of the Etruscan empire. Chimaera of Arezzo. Architectural terracottas of Orvieto and Falerii.
423	In Campania, Capua is captured by the Samnites.
End of 5th century	Celtic invaders enter northern and then central Italy.

IV – 4th and Early 3rd Centuries: the Roman Conquest and the End of Etruscan Independence

396	Capture of Veii by the Romans after a ten years' siege.
390	The Gauls reach Rome, which is captured and set on fire. Priests and sacred objects from Rome find safety in Caere, which thereafter is granted special privileges.
384	The Syracusan fleet raids Pyrgi, the port of Caere, and plunders the Etruscan federal shrine, dedicated to Uni (the Etruscan Juno).
350	Conquest of Padan Etruria by the Gauls; capture of Felsina (Bologna), the chief town.

First half of 4th century	Stelae depicting fighting with Celts (Bologna).
Second half of 4th century	Rome at war with Tarquinia, Arezzo and Perugia. The Etruscan cities are conquered one by one after various risings and wars. Painted tombs of Tarquinia and Orvieto. François Tomb, Vulci.
308	Defeat of Tarquinia.
273	Foundation of a Latin colony at Cosa (near Orbetello).
265	Capture and destruction of Volsinii, the last of the Etruscan cities.
First half of 3rd century	Sarcophagus of Torre San Severo (near Orvieto). Second Tomba dell'Orco and Tomba del Cardinale, Tarquinia.

V – Roman Etruria

264–241	First Punic War.
225	The Romans and their Etruscan allies defeat the Gauls at Telamon.
218–201	Second Punic War.
End of 3rd century	Roman victory over the Gauls in the Po valley. Terracotta pediment, Telamon. The Capitoline Brutus. Terracottas from Arezzo. Terracotta sarcophagi of Tuscania.
2nd century	Establishment of many Roman colonies in the Po valley.

189	Foundation of the colony of Bononia (Bologna) on the site of the Etruscan Felsina.
146	Destruction of Carthage and of Corinth.
1st century	A number of Etruscan towns take part in the Civil Wars. Sulla deprives Volterra and Arezzo of their right to vote and confiscates part of their territory. Small funerary urns of Volterra; the large bronze statues of the "Arringatore".
88	After the Social War the Etruscans are granted Roman citizenship.
42	Perugia is besieged and set on fire by Octavius.

LIST OF ILLUSTRATIONS

18 *Villanovan razors of half-moon shape. From Vulci. 8th century B.C. Villa Giulia Museum, Rome.*

19 *Bronze strigil with female statuette on handle. From Praeneste. 3rd century B.C. Villa Giulia Museum, Rome.*

20 *The same: detail.*

21 *Villanovan bronze fibula of "serpent" type with facing of silver. From Vulci. Beginning of 7th century B.C. Villa Giulia Museum, Rome.*

22 *The same.*

23 *Villanovan bronze fibula of "serpent" type with disc. From Vulci. 8th century B.C. Villa Giulia Museum, Rome.*

24 *Impasto vase with numerous mouths. Beginning of 7th century B.C. Tarquinia Museum.*

25 *Bronze situla with double handle. From Barbarano. 3rd century B.C. Villa Giulia Museum, Rome.*

26 *Bronze head of young man. From Cagli (Marche). Height 22 cm. Beginning of 4th century B.C. Villa Giulia Museum, Rome.*

27 *Terracotta head, life size, of the god Hermes. One of the acroteria from the* columen *of the temple of Apollo at Veii. About 500 B.C. Villa Giulia Museum, Rome.*

28 *Polychrome terracotta statue of Apollo, life size, by the sculptor Vulca. From Veii. About 500 B.C. Villa Giulia Museum, Rome.*

29 *The same: detail of head.*

30 *Polychrome terracotta head of a helmeted warrior. From Conca (Satricum). About 500 B.C. Villa Giulia Museum, Rome.*

31 *Terracotta head of a dead warrior from the pediment of the temple of Mater Matuta at Conca (Satricum). About 500 B.C. Villa Giulia Museum, Rome.*

32 *Terracotta head of a warrior. Decorative element from a building. From Veii. 5th century B.C. Villa Giulia Museum, Rome.*

33 *Stone head of a woman wearing a torque, originally at the entrance to a tomb. Height 46 cm. From Orvieto. First half of 3rd century B.C. Barracco Museum, Rome. (Ph. G. Franceschi).*

34 *Terracotta figure of a girl combing her hair. From Solaia, near Sarteano. About 100 B.C. Florence Museum. (Ph. G. Franceschi).*

35 *Terracotta head of a man. From Cerveteri. Hellenistic period. Villa Giulia Museum, Rome.*

36 *Polychrome antefix of a Gorgon's head. From Veii. About 500 B.C. Villa Giulia Museum, Rome.*

37 *Terracotta model of a small temple with a single cella. Height 21.5 cm. From Vulci. Hellenistic period. Villa Giulia Museum, Rome.*

38 *Terracotta model of a house. Height 27 cm. From Velletri. Hellenistic period. Villa Giulia Museum, Rome.*

39 *Terracotta model of the pediment of an Etruscan temple. From Nemi. About 300 B.C. Villa Giulia Museum, Rome.*

40 *Terracotta model of a pillared building. Height 15 cm. From Vulci. Hellenistic period. Villa Giulia Museum, Rome.*

41 *Architectural terracotta representing a procession of chariots and warriors. From Praeneste. First half of 6th century B.C. Villa Giulia Museum, Rome.*

42 *Chariot race: bas-relief from a stone cippus. From Chiusi. About 470 B.C. Palermo Museum. (Ph. Museum).*

43 *Stone sculpture of a man on a sea monster. From Vulci. End of 7th century B.C. Villa Giulia Museum, Rome.*

44 *Terracotta acroterion from the temple of Sassi Caduti, Cività Castellana (Falerii Veteres). Beginning of 5th century B.C. Villa Giulia Museum, Rome.*

45 *Stone centaur. From Vulci. About 600 B.C. Villa Giulia Museum, Rome.*

46 *Terracotta group of winged horses (originally harnessed to a chariot). Architectural decoration from a temple at Tarquinia. About 300 B.C. Tarquinia Museum.*

47 *Silver gilt cup, in the orientalising style with concentric rings of Egyptian-style motifs. From the Bernardini Tomb, Praeneste. 7th century B.C. Villa Giulia Museum, Rome.*

48 *Large silver gilt vase decorated with six snake protomes. From the Bernardini Tomb, Praeneste. Middle of 7th century B.C. Villa Giulia Museum, Rome.*

49 *Large gold pectoral in the orientalising style: long lines of fantastic animals modelled in the round. From the Barberini Tomb, Praeneste. Middle of 7th century B.C. Villa Giulia Museum, Rome.*

50 *Gold pectoral similar to the one from the Barberini Tomb. From the Bernardini Tomb, Praeneste. Middle of 7th century B.C. Villa Giulia Museum, Rome.*

51 *Etruscan inscription on a sheet of gold, found in 1964 in the shrine of Uni (the Etruscan Juno) at Pyrgi. About 500 B.C. Villa Giulia Museum, Rome. (Ph. Museum).*

52 *The same.*

53 *Punic inscription on a sheet of gold, found in the sanctuary of Uni at Pyrgi. In this the goddess is worshipped under the name of Astarte. About 500 B.C. Villa Giulia Museum, Rome. (Ph. Museum).*

54 *Ivory horse's head. From the Barberini Tomb, Praeneste. Middle of 7th century B.C. Villa Giulia Museum, Rome.*

55 *Ivory ornament from a casket, representing a warrior drawn by a lion. From the Bernardini Tomb, Praeneste. Middle of 7th century B.C. Villa Giulia Museum, Rome.*

56 *Necklaces made of small perforated bronze tubes. From Vulci. Villa Giulia Museum, Rome.*

57 *Necklace of 40 amber beads. From Vulci. Villa Giulia Museum, Rome.*

58 *Ivory handle of a fan or mirror in the form of a hand and fore-arm. From the Bernardini Tomb, Praeneste. About 650 B.C. Villa Giulia Museum, Rome.*

59 *A funeral road in the necropolis of Cerveteri.*

60 *The same.*

61 *The same.*

62 *Part of the area of large tumuli in the necropolis of Cerveteri.*

63 *Large tumulus in the necropolis of Cerveteri.*

64 *Air photograph of the necropolis of Monte Abbatone, Cerveteri. Taken by the R.A.F. during the second world war. (Ph. C.M. Lerici, Rome).*

65 *Tomba della Capanna, Cerveteri. 7th century B.C.*

66 *Tomba degli Scudi e Sedie, Cerveteri. 6th century B.C.*

67 *Detail of architecture of the Tomb of the Painted Lions, Cerveteri. 6th century B.C.*

68 *Interior of the Tomb of the Painted Lions, Cerveteri. 6th century B.C.*

69 *Detail of architecture of the Tomb of the Alcove, Cerveteri. 4th-3rd centuries B.C.*

70 *Tomb of the Alcove, Cerveteri. 4th-3rd centuries B.C.*

71 *Instrument for measuring the electrical resistivity of the soil. By noting and studying anomalies recorded by this instrument it is possible to locate tombs under the ground. (Ph. C.M. Lerici, Rome).*

72 *The proton magnetometer. This recently developed geophysical instrument measures the intensity of the magnetic field at a particular point, and variations in the field make it possible to locate tombs. (Ph. C.M. Lerici, Rome).*

73 *Periscope developed by C.M. Lerici for inspecting the interior of tombs without excavation. (Ph. C.M. Lerici, Rome).*

74 *Photographic probe which makes it possible to take photographs of the interior of an unexcavated tomb. (Ph. C.M. Lerici, Rome).*

75 *Photographs of the Bartoccini Tomb at Tarquinia, taken with the Lerici photographic probe. (Ph. C.M. Lerici, Rome).*

76–79 *Tomb of the Bulls, Tarquinia. About 540 B.C.*

80 *Tomb of the Baron: conversation between a woman and two young men with horses. Tarquinia. About 510 B.C.*

81 *Tomb of the Baron: conversation between two young men with horses. Tarquinia. About 510 B.C.*

82 *Tomb of the Baron: a libation scene. Tarquinia. About 510 B.C.*

83 *Tomb of the Augurs: a masked dancer ("Phersu"). Tarquinia. About 530 B.C.*

98 *Tomb of the Triclinium. About 470 B.C. Tarquinia Museum.*

99 *Tomb of the Triclinium: dancer. About 470 B.C. Tarquinia Museum.*

100 *Tomba dell'Orco: Polyphemus blinded by Odysseus. Tarquinia. Later part of the tomb: 3rd or 2nd century B.C.*

101 *Tomba dell'Orco: the monster Geryon. Tarquinia. Later part of the tomb: 3rd or 2nd century B.C.*

102 *Tomba dell'Orco: Tiresias and Agamemnon. Tarquinia. Later part of the tomb: 3rd or 2nd century B.C.*

103 *Tomba dell'Orco: winged demon, serving boy and vases. Tarquinia. Later part of the tomb: 3rd or 2nd century B.C.*

104 *Tomba dell'Orco: head of a woman. Tarquinia. Older part of the tomb: end of 4th century B.C.*

105 *Head and shoulders of a baby in swaddling clothes. Votive terracotta. From Vulci. Hellenistic period. Villa Giulia Museum, Rome.*

106 *Baby in swaddling clothes. Votive terracotta. From Vulci. Hellenistic period. Villa Giulia Museum, Rome.*

107 *Villanovan hut-urn (terracotta). From Vulci. 8th century B.C. Villa Giulia Museum, Rome.*

108 *Terracotta sarcophagus: husband and wife on funeral couch. From Cerveteri. About 530 B.C. Louvre, Paris. (Ph. Museum).*

109 *Terracotta sarcophagus: husband and wife on funeral couch. From Cerveteri. About 530 B.C. Villa Giulia Museum, Rome.*

110 *The same: detail.*

111 *Bronze cinerary urn in the shape of a house. From Cività Castellana. 7th century B.C. Villa Giulia Museum, Rome.*

112 *Bucchero oenochoë with trilobate spout and relief ornament. From Vulci. 6th century B.C. Villa Giulia Museum, Rome.*

113 *Oenochoë of* bucchero pesante *with relief ornament. 6th century B.C. Tarquinia Museum.*

114 *Villanovan ossuary of impasto with lid in the form of a helmet. From Vulci. 8th century B.C. Villa Giulia Museum, Rome.*

115 *Bucchero* kyathos *with vertical handle. From Vulci. 8th century B.C. Tarquinia Museum.*

116 *Bucchero* kyathos *with vertical handle. From Vulci. 7th century B.C. Villa Giulia Museum, Rome.*

117 *Bucchero oenochoë with disc ornaments on handle. 7th century B.C. Tarquinia Museum.*

118 *Bucchero oenochoë with trilobate spout. 6th century B.C. Villa Giulia Museum, Rome.*

119 *Bucchero situla with superimposed bands of decoration. From Cerveteri. 7th-6th centuries B.C. Villa Giulia Museum, Rome.*

120 *Bucchero cup with elaborate base. 6th century B.C. Tarquinia Museum.*

121 *Impasto jug with ribbed surface. 7th century B.C. Tarquinia Museum.*

122 *Griffin's head (terracotta). From Cività Castellana. 7th century B.C. Villa Giulia Museum, Rome.*

123 *Griffin's head (terracotta). From Cività Castellana. 7th century B.C. Villa Giulia Museum, Rome.*

124 *Impasto jugs with incised decoration. From Cività Castellana. 7th century B.C. Villa Giulia Museum, Rome.*

125 *Bucchero pedestal cup with elaborate plastic ornament. 6th century B.C. Villa Giulia Museum, Rome.*

126 *Etruscan* krater *with pillared handles and black-figure painting. Second half of 6th century B.C. Tarquinia Museum.*

127 *Etruscan black-figure amphora. Second half of 6th century B.C. Tarquinia Museum.*

128 *Italo-geometric oenochoë with painted decoration. First half of 7th century B.C. Tarquinia Museum.*

129 *Italo-geometric oenochoë with painted decoration. First half of 7th century B.C. Tarquinia Museum.*

130 *Italo-geometric jar. First half of 7th century B.C. Tarquinia Museum.*

131 *Bucchero amphora with relief ornament. 6th century B.C. Hermitage Museum, Leningrad.*

132 *Painted dish with figure of a fighting elephant. 3rd century B.C. Villa Giulia Museum, Rome.*

(Except where otherwise indicated, all the photographs were taken by Gérard Bertin, Genève,)

INDEX

Printed in Switzerland

THE TEXT AND ILLUSTRATIONS
IN THIS VOLUME WERE PRINTED
ON THE PRESSES OF NAGEL
PUBLISHERS IN GENEVA

FINISHED IN APRIL 1969
BINDING BY NAGEL PUBLISHERS,
GENEVA

OFFSET COLOUR SEPARATION EXECUTED BY
PHOTO-CHROMO-GRAVURE, LYONS
AND BY PHOTOLITHOS ARGRAF, GENEVA

LEGAL DEPOSIT No 481

PRINTED IN SWITZERLAND

VENETI
Mantua
Atria
Parma
Mutina
Spina
Genoa
Casalecchio
Felsina
Ravenna
Marzabotto
ADRIATIC
SEA
Luni
LIGURIANS
Ariminum
Montemurlo
S. Agata
Londa
Sieve
Verucchio
Auser
Trebbio
Quinto
Fiesole
M. Falterona
Florence
Traviglione
Pisa
LIGURIAN SEA
Antella
UMBRIANS
Arno
Elsa
Esa
Panzano
Ancona
Terricciole
Quercianella
Laiatico
Castellina Chianti
Arezzo
Casaglia
Castiglioncello
Cecina
Cerreta
Volterra
Mezzavia
Vada
Marciano
Sodo
Monteriggioni
Montescudaio
Pomarance
Brolio
Cortona
Tiber
Casale
S. Francesco
Camucia
Betolle
Castel
Perugia
S. Vincenzo
Massa Marittima
Chinciano
S. Mariano
Chiusi
Dolciano
Palazzone